FEAST OF FLAVOURS
from the Japanese Kitchen

FEAST OF FLAVOURS from the Japanese Kitchen

A STEP-BY-STEP CULINARY ADVENTURE

Keiko Ishida

Dedication and Acknowledgements

I dedicate this book to my mother, Takako Hamanaka, and my husband, Takehisa, who are always incredibly supportive of me. I wish to thank my culinary friends, Susan Utama, Low Siew Khee, Chen Mei Ling Emily, Lin Limei, Elisabeth Lindh, Patricia Nano and Loke Kah Yin; I am really fortunate to have them as friends. I also thank Shermay Lee who has provided me with many opportunities to showcase my cooking and baking here in Singapore, and Catherine Swann, my English teacher and close neighbour. Last but not least, I thank Junko Suzuki for her kindness and assistance in my kitchen during the photography session.
I am very happy to have this opportunity to share my passion for Japanese cooking and culture in this book, and sincerely hope that you will delight in sharing my recipes with your family and friends too.

– Keiko Ishida

Photographer: Allan Tan, Flowerchild Projekts
Editor: Selina Lim Siew Lin
Designer: Lock Hong Liang

Copyright © 2007 Marshall Cavendish International (Asia) Private Limited

Published by Marshall Cavendish Cuisine
An imprint of Marshall Cavendish International
1 New Industrial Road, Singapore 536196

All rights reserved

No part of this publication may be reproduced, stored in a retrieval system or transmitted, in any form or by any means, electronic, mechanical, photocopying, recording or otherwise, without the prior permission of the copyright owner. Request for permission should be addressed to the Publisher, Marshall Cavendish International (Asia) Private Limited, 1 New Industrial Road, Singapore 536196. Tel: (65) 6213 9300, fax: (65) 6285 4871. E-mail: genref@sg.marshallcavendish.com. Online bookstore:www.marshallcavendish.com/genref.

Limits of Liability/Disclaimer of Warranty: The Author and Publisher of this book have used their best efforts in preparing this book. The Publisher makes no representation or warranties with respect to the contents of this book and is not responsible for the outcome of any recipe in this book. While the Publisher has reviewed each recipe carefully, the reader may not always achieve the results desired due to variations in ingredients, cooking temperatures and individual cooking abilities. The Publisher shall in no event be liable for any loss of profit or any other commercial damage, including but not limited to special, incidental, consequential, or other damages.

Other Marshall Cavendish Offices:

Marshall Cavendish Ltd. 119 Wardour Street, London W1F 0UW, UK • Marshall Cavendish Corporation. 99 White Plains Road, Tarrytown NY 10591-9001, USA • Marshall Cavendish International (Thailand) Co Ltd. 253 Asoke, 12th Flr, Sukhumvit 21 Road, Klongtoey Nua, Wattana, Bangkok 10110, Thailand • Marshall Cavendish (Malaysia) Sdn Bhd, Times Subang, Lot 46, Subang Hi-Tech Industrial Park, Batu Tiga, 40000 Shah Alam, Selangor Darul Ehsan, Malaysia

Marshall Cavendish is a trademark of Times Publishing Limited

National Library Board Singapore Cataloguing in Publication Data

Ishida, Keiko, 1965-
Feast of flavours from the Japanese kitchen : a step-by-step culinary adventure / Keiko Ishida. – Singapore : Marshall Cavendish Cuisine, c2007.
p. cm. – (Feast of flavours)
Includes index.
ISBN-13 : 978-981-261-415-5
ISBN-10 : 981-261-415-X

1. Cookery, Japanese. I. Title. II. Series: Feast of flavours

TX724.5.J3
641.5952 -- dc22   SLS2007016069

Printed in Singapore by Times Graphics Pte Ltd

CONTENTS

Introduction
- 6   Cooking Techniques
- 8   Cooking Utensils
- 13   Weights & Measures

Soups
- 16   Bean Curd and Seaweed Miso Soup (*Tofu To Wakame No Misoshiru*)
- 19   Miso Soup with Pork and Vegetables (*Ton Jiru*)
- 21   Tokyo-Style New Year's Soup (*Ozo-Ni Kanto Style*)
- 22   Short-neck Clam Clear Soup (*Asari No Osumashi*)

Side Dishes
- 26   Cucumber and Octopus Salad with Sweet Vinegar Dressing (*Kyuri To Tako No Sunomono*)
- 29   Deep-Fried Bean Curd (*Agedashi Tofu*)
- 31   Savoury Egg Custard (*Chawan Mushi*)
- 32   Simmered Hijiki Seaweed (*Hijiki No Nimono*)
- 34   Vegetables with Bean Curd Dressing (*Yasai No Shira Ae*)

Vegetables
- 38   Simmered Chinese Flowering Cabbage and Deep-Fried Bean Curd (*Komatsuna To Age No Nibitashi*)
- 41   Pan-Fried Aubergines with Miso Sauce (*Nasu No Nabeshigi*)
- 42   Simmered Lotus Root (*Renkon No Kimpira*)
- 45   French Beans with Sesame Dressing (*Ingen No Goma Ae*)
- 46   Simmered Pumpkin (*Kabocha No Amani*)
- 49   Simmered Radish with Minced Chicken (*Daikon No Soboro Ni*)
- 50   Simmered Vegetables and Chicken (*Chikuzen Ni*)

Seafood
- 54   Broiled Yellowtail (*Buri no Nabeteri*)
- 57   Grilled Spanish Mackerel with White Miso Paste (*Sawara No Saikyo Yaki*)
- 59   Salt-Grilled Horse Mackerel (*Aji No Shio Yaki*)
- 61   Simmered Mackerel in Grated Radish (*Saba No Mizore Ni*)
- 62   Simmered Red Snapper (*Tai No Nitsuke*)
- 65   Simmered Squid and Taro (*Ika To Satoimo No Nimono*)
- 67   Deep-Fried Seafood and Vegetables (*Tempura*)

Meat & Poultry
- 70   Braised Beef and Potatoes (*Niku Jaga*)
- 73   Braised Pork (*Buta No Kakuni*)
- 75   Japanese-Style Deep-Fried Chicken (*Tori No Tatsuta Age*)
- 77   Pan-Fried Ginger Pork (*Buta No Shoga Yaki*)
- 78   Deep-Fried Breaded Pork Cutlets (*Ton Katsu*)
- 81   Teriyaki Chicken (*Tori No Teriyaki*)

Rice & Noodles
- 84   Chicken and Eggs On Rice (*Oyako Don*)
- 87   Cold Buckwheat Noodles (*Zaru Soba*)
- 89   Deep-Fried Bean Curd Stuffed with Vinegared Rice (*Inari Sushi*)
- 90   Mixed Rice (*Maze Gohan*)
- 92   Sukiyaki Beef Bowl (*Gyu Don*)
- 95   Red Rice (*Seki Han*)
- 96   Thick-Rolled Sushi (*Futomaki Sushi*)

Desserts
- 100   Rice Balls with Red Bean Paste (*Ohagi*)
- 103   Candied Sweet Potatoes (*Daigaku Imo*)
- 105   Green Tea and Brown Sugar Buns (*Matcha To Kokuto Manju*)
- 106   Rice Balls Skewers (*Mitarashi Dango*)
- 108   Agar-agar, Glutinous Rice Balls and Red Bean Paste with Syrup (*Shiratama Ann Mitsu*)
- 110   Pancakes with Red Bean Paste (*Dora Yaki*)

Glossary & Index
- 114   Glossary of Ingredients
- 122   Index

INTRODUCTION

COOKING TECHNIQUES

A lot of water is used in Japanese cooking, and this is partly related to the topography and eco-system of Japan, which provides an excellent water source of premium quality.

A long strip of island that stretches from the north to the south, Japan comprises many mountains in the central part, and a few fertile plains between the mountains and the sea. The large, fertile forests on the mountains, that make up the beginning of the water cycle, are regarded as national treasures.

When rain falls, the minerals from the mountains are washed down into the soil of the plains, enabling the cultivation of rice and other important crops, vegetables and fruit. This mineral-rich water also flows into the sea from the rivers and streams, resulting in pristine waters around the coastal areas.

Marine life of all varieties come and feed in this water that is full of rich minerals and plankton. With this natural abundance of marine life, fresh seafood and seaweed of countless varieties have become an important part of the Japanese diet over time.

Since the key to Japanese cooking is the use of ultra-fresh ingredients, cooking methods are kept very simple to bring out the best of their natural flavours. Many cooking methods involve the use of water, including blanching, boiling, simmering and steaming.

Blanching / Boiling

Blanching and boiling are cooking methods that help soften ingredients, remove any bitter tastes, as well as enable the ingredients to absorb seasoning easily, and retain their colour. When blanching or boiling ingredients, use plenty of water to enable them to cook evenly.

Blanching is usually employed for delicate ingredients that require only light cooking, or will be subjected to further cooking. Green vegetables like spinach, asparagus and peas should be cooked briefly in salted water that has been brought to the boil first, then drained and soaked in ice water, or cooled on a flat sieve, using a hand fan to refresh the vegetables.

As for hardy root vegetables such as whole or large chunks of carrots, radishes and potatoes that require a longer cooking time, immerse them in cold water, then heat and bring to the boil until cooked. For root vegetables that have been cut into small pieces, they can be cooked directly in boiling water, as they do not require a long cooking time.

Steaming

In Japan, steaming is a traditional cooking method that has been used for more then a thousand years. The ingredients are cooked by the hot steam that rises from the boiling water below. In this way, excess moisture is forced out of the steamed ingredients and the food retains their natural flavours to the maximum, as they do not come into direct contact with the boiling water.

To steam food, place them in a heatproof (flameproof) container or steaming rack, and place over boiling water, then cover tightly to retain the steam (heat) to cook the food.

However, for ingredients with a natural bitter taste, such as leafy greens like spinach, it is better to blanch them, as the bitterness is then leached into the water. I recommend using a round-shaped steamer instead of a square-shaped one; it distributes heat more evenly, and provides higher pressure to cook the food more quickly.

Simmering

In Japanese cooking, ingredients are usually simmered in dashi, to which seasoning has been added. First of all, sugar, sake and mirin are added, followed by soy sauce and salt at a later stage. Salt is always added after sugar; it is believed that salt has a more refined texture than sugar, and is therefore more easily absorbed by ingredients to accentuate their flavours.

To make a good simmered dish, always choose the freshest ingredients and parboil, or precook them, before simmering in a top-quality dashi. However, do note that fish is always simmered in water, and not dashi, since the latter is basically a stock made from fish and seaweed; the fish dish will become overpoweringly fishy if dashi is used.

As the liquid for simmering ingredients in, is usually a relatively small amount, it is important to select a pan, or pot of the correct size that will allow the ingredients to be just covered by the simmering liquid. Too large a pan will produce a simmered dish that is not fully flavoured.

A drop-in lid is also a very useful item for use when simmering. The lid is placed directly over the ingredients to hold them in place, and prevent them from breaking up. This will allow the ingredients to cook evenly in a small amount of stock, and prevent the stock from evaporating too quickly. If a drop-in lid is not available, a sheet of baking paper or aluminium foil, cut into the right shape and size will do as well.

Grilling (Broiling)

Nearly every Japanese home kitchen has both a gas and fish griller, as the Japanese love to eat grilled fish. Dried and semi-dried fish, marinated fish and, of course, fresh fish are staples in Japan. Grilled food is popular, as they are quick and easy to prepare. When grilling fresh fish, always sprinkle with salt (natural mineral salt is preferred) before grilling, and grill the serving side first, before grilling the other side.

A typical marinade or glazing sauce for grilled foods includes blending sake, mirin , sugar and soy sauce together. Fish or meats are first marinated in this seasoning and then grilled, basting with the sauce regularly while cooking.

However, I prefer to use a heavy-based pan over the stove to grill my foods at home, as pans are easier to clean after cooking, and the foods are also less likely to burn, as it is far easier to regulate the heat over the stove.

Deep-frying

Deep-frying has become a common cooking method in Japan, with the popularity of tempura, which was first introduced from the West, about 400 years ago. Since the boiling point of oil is higher than water, ingredients can be cooked quickly this way. Always deep-fry ingredients in small batches, as deep-frying large quantities at one go may cause the temperature of the oil to drop too quickly, resulting in fried food which is soggy, and unevenly cooked.

COOKING UTENSILS

Drop-in Lid (*Otoshi Buta*)
This is a utensil unique to Japanese cooking. Wooden and light stainless steel drop-in lids are available. Used when preparing simmered dishes, the lid fits right into the pan to rest on top of the ingredients directly. Because they are lighter, wooden drop-in lids are especially handy when cooking fragile ingredients such as soft bean curd and vegetables. Using a drop-in lid also prevents the ingredients from shifting and, hence, losing their shape as the lid keeps them in place during cooking. Perpetually "bathed" in seasoning during cooking, the simmered dishes turn out more flavourful than usual. Always soak wooden drop-in lids in water before use. If a drop-in lid is not available, fold or trim a sheet of aluminium foil or baking paper to fit into the pan, and use it as a disposable lid.

Kitchen Chopsticks (*Sai Bashi*)
Kitchen chopsticks are indispensable tools in Japanese cooking that are used for many purposes, from stir-frying, to beating eggs and turning small food items over during pan-frying. In general, the chopsticks vary in length according to the various functions they serve. For example, long chopsticks are usually reserved for deep-frying foods and to keep the hands as far away from spluttering hot oil as possible. Medium-length chopsticks are used for general tasks, such as gentle stir-frying and beating eggs.

Ladle with Sieve (*Aku Sukui*)
A very useful utensil in the kitchen, this small sieve is used for skimming off foam that rises to the surface of boiling liquids, such as soups and stews. It is also good for straining small pieces of solid ingredients from soups.

Earthenware Pot (*Do Nabe*)
Made from clay, this pot retains heat well and also allows heat to transfer slowly and gently. It is therefore ideal for cooking hotpot dishes and soups, such as steamboat, *shabu shabu* and *yose nabe*. It is also used for cooking rice and noodle dishes. After using, always cool the earthenware pot completely before washing and do not heat the pot without any liquid in it; the pot may crack.

Miso Strainer (*Miso Koshi*)
This is a twin-set utensil, used specifically for adding soy bean or miso paste to soups evenly, to create a smooth-textured soup. The miso paste is placed in a small but deep metal-mesh basket which is then submerged in the soup. The miso paste is rubbed into the liquid with the small perforated ladle attached.

Grater (*Oroshi Gane*)
Graters are made from a variety of materials including copper, stainless steel, plastic, aluminium and ceramic. Whatever the material the grater is made of, it basically has a flat surface with many fine spikes, or a combination of tiny spikes and holes. While a coarse grater is used for grating hardy vegetables such as white radish (*daikon*) and carrots, a fine grater is used for grating dense spices including fresh garlic, wasabi and ginger.

Wooden Sushi Tub (*Han Dai*)
This is a large wooden tub for mixing cooked rice with vinegar dressing to prepare the rice for sushi. It is usually made from swara cypress wood, which is capable of absorbing moisture. Always soak the tub in water for a few minutes before use; a dry tub willl cause the rice to stick to it, and the vinegar dressing to be absorbed by the wood. Just before preparing the rice for sushi, drain and wipe with a damp cloth. After use, wash the tub well with water and air-dry before storing. Although the sushi tub is extremely useful if you are making sushi on a regular basis, a large mixing bowl made of stainless steel, plastic or glass is equally ideal.

Bamboo Mat (*Makisu*)
Typically measuring about 22 x 20-cm (9 x 8-in), the bamboo mat is a must-have for making sushi rolls. It is better to choose a mat that comprises many small bamboo sticks threaded together to form a flat surface on one side, than one which is made of less, but larger pieces, as the former is more flexible and makes sushi-rolling easier. Bamboo mats, especially those with round bamboo sticks threaded together, can also be used for shaping and creating line patterns on thick-rolled omelettes. After using, ensure that your mat is clean, and completely dry before storing, or it will turn mouldy.

Grinding Bowl and Pestle (*Suribachi & Surikogi*)

A earthenware bowl that comes in various sizes, the Japanese grinding bowl can be differentiated from the usual grinding bowl with its numerous sharp ridges on the inside surface. This feature makes it highly effective for grinding small ingredients including spices and sesame seeds into fine pastes, as well as mashing and pounding malleable items like rice dough, with a wooden pestle.

Omelette Pan (*Tamago Yaki Nabe*)

The Japanese omelette pan is a rectangular frying pan that is used specifically for making thick-rolled omelettes. Professional chefs use a traditional rectangular pan that is made of copper and plated with tin on the inside. However, for the purposes of easy home cooking, a non-stick rectangular pan, or a regular frying pan is recommended, as it is easier to cook in and maintain. If using a non-stick frying pan, simply trim the edges of the cooked omelette to obtain a rectangular shape.

Oyako Pan (*Oyako Nabe*)

An *oyako* pan is a unique-looking small pan, specially designed for preparing *donburi* (rice) dishes, which are served in deep ceramic bowls. With a diameter of about 15 cm (6 in), the round pan allows the preparation of only a single serve at any one time. The handle is attached to the pan at a right angle, making it relatively easy to hold and "slide" the simmered dish directly onto rice in a single-serve bowl.

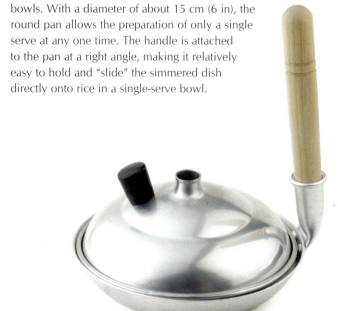

Flat Sieve (*Bon Zaru*)

Made of bamboo or stainless steel, the flat sieve can be used for straining a wide variety of ingredients including noodles and beans, and cooling or air-drying ingredients such as vegetables after cooking. Wash carefully and air-dry completely before storing.

WEIGHTS & MEASURES

Quantities for this book are given in Metric and American (spoon and cup) measures. Standard spoon and cup measurements used are: 1 teaspoon = 5 ml, 1 dessertspoon = 10 ml, 1 tablespoon = 15 ml, 1 cup = 250 ml. All measures are level unless otherwise stated.

LIQUID AND VOLUME MEASURES

Metric	Imperial	American
5 ml	1/6 fl oz	1 teaspoon
10 ml	1/3 fl oz	1 dessertspoon
15 ml	1/2 fl oz	1 tablespoon
60 ml	2 fl oz	1/4 cup (4 tablespoons)
85 ml	2 1/2 fl oz	1/3 cup
90 ml	3 fl oz	3/8 cup (6 tablespoons)
125 ml	4 fl oz	1/2 cup
180 ml	6 fl oz	3/4 cup
250 ml	8 fl oz	1 cup
300 ml	10 fl oz (1/2 pint)	1 1/4 cup
375 ml	12 fl oz	1 1/2 cup
435 ml	14 fl oz	1 3/4 cup
500 ml	16 fl oz	2 cups
625 ml	20 fl oz (1 pint)	2 1/2 cups
750 ml	24 fl oz (1 1/5 pint)	3 cups
1 litre	32 fl oz (1 3/5 pint)	4 cups
1.25 litres	40 fl oz (2 pints)	5 cups
1.5 litres	48 fl oz (2 2/5 pints)	6 cups
2.5 litres	80 fl oz (4 pints)	10 cups

DRY MEASURES

Metric	Imperial
30 g	1 oz
45 g	1 1/2 oz
55 g	2 oz
70 g	2 1/2 oz
85 g	3 oz
100 g	3 1/2 oz
110 g	4 oz
125 g	4 1/2 oz
140 g	5 oz
280 g	10 oz
450 g	16 oz (1 lb)
500 g	1 lb, 1 1/2 oz
700 g	1 1/2 lb
800 g	1 3/4 lb
1 kg	2 lb, 3 oz
1.5 kg	3 lb, 4 1/2 oz
2 kg	4 lb, 6 oz

LENGTH

Metric	Imperial
0.5 cm	1/4 in
1 cm	1/2 in
1.5 cm	3/4 in
2.5 cm	1 in

OVEN TEMPERATURE

	°C	°F	Gas Regulo
Very slow	120	250	1
Slow	150	300	2
Moderately slow	160	325	3
Moderate	180	350	4
Moderately hot	190/200	370/400	5/6
Hot	210/220	410/440	6/7
Very hot	230	450	8
Super hot	250/290	475/550	9/10

ABBREVIATION

Tbsp	tablespoon
tsp	teaspoon
kg	kilogram
g	gram
l	litres
ml	millilitres

Bean Curd and Seaweed Miso Soup (*Tofu To Wakame No Misoshiru*)

Miso Soup with Pork and Vegetables (*Ton Jiru*)

Tokyo-Style New Year's Soup (*Ozo-Ni Kanto Style*)

Short-neck Clam Clear Soup (*Asari No Osumashi*)

SOUPS

BEAN CURD AND SEAWEED MISO SOUP
(TOFU TO WAKAME NO MISOSHIRU)

Served at most meals, steamed rice and miso soup are the traditional staples of Japanese cuisine. For an interesting variation to this recipe, substitute the dried seaweed with vegetables such as ladyfingers, mushrooms, snow peas or chives, or, use deep-fried bean curd, potatoes, bamboo shoots or white radish to replace regular bean curd.

Ingredients

Bean curd (soft or firm)	200 g (7 oz), cut into small cubes
Dried cut seaweed (*wakame*)	1 Tbsp
Soy bean paste (*miso*)	60 g (2 oz)
Japanese spring onion (*naga negi* / scallion)	¼, finely sliced

Dashi (see Note)

Water	800 ml (26 fl oz / 3¼ cups)
Dried kelp (*konbu*)	10-cm (4-in) piece
Bonito flakes	25 g (1 oz)

Step-By-Step

When preparing dashi, add bonito flakes to water that is just boiling, then reduce heat to simmer for a few seconds.

Place a flat metal sieve over a large pot, lined with a piece of clean cloth. Carefully strain dashi.

Place soy bean paste into a miso strainer. Rub soy bean paste through sieve into soup to dissolve completely, and achieve a smooth-textured soup.

Note: To save time when cooking, make an instant stock by dissolving 1⅓ tsp dashi powder in 700 ml (22 fl oz / 2¾ cups) water.

Method

- Prepare dashi. Put water and kelp into a saucepan and leave for 30 minutes. Place over medium heat and when small bubbles appear from the bottom, remove kelp.
- When water is boiling, add bonito flakes, then reduce heat and simmer for a few seconds. Remove from heat, then leave until bonito flakes sink to the bottom of saucepan. Strain stock and discard solids.
- Return strained stock to the saucepan and add bean curd and seaweed. Bring to the boil, then remove from heat. Strain soy bean paste into soup, then stir until bean paste has dissolved.
- Reheat soup and return to the boil, then remove from heat immediately. Garnish with sliced spring onion and serve hot.

MISO SOUP WITH PORK AND VEGETABLES
(TON JIRU)

In Japanese, *ton* refers to "pork". Substantial enough to be served as a main dish, this speciality originates from northern Japan, and is traditionally served at festivities held by the riverside during autumn.

Ingredients

Sesame oil	2 Tbsp
Thinly-sliced pork belly or pork shoulder	150 g (5$\frac{1}{3}$ oz), cut into bite-size pieces
Potatoes	2, small, peeled, cut into cubes, then soaked and drained just before use
Carrot	$\frac{1}{2}$, peeled and thinly sliced
White radish (*daikon*)	6-cm (2$\frac{1}{2}$-in) length, peeled and thinly sliced
White devil's tongue jelly (*konnyaku*), packed in water	130 g (4$\frac{1}{2}$ oz), drained, cut into thick matchsticks, then blanched and drained
Burdock (*gobo*)	70g (2$\frac{1}{2}$ oz), scrubbed clean and cut into small pieces
Fresh shiitake mushrooms	2, stems discarded and thinly sliced
Deep-dried bean curd (*abura age*)	1, cut into thin strips
Sake	2 Tbsp
Soy bean paste (*miso*)	60–70 g (2–2$\frac{1}{2}$ oz)
Japanese spring onion (*naga negi* / scallion)	1, finely sliced

Dashi (see Note)

Water	1 litre (32 fl oz / 4 cups)
Dried kelp (*konbu*)	12-cm (5-in) piece
Bonito flakes	30 g (1 oz)

Garnishing

Chopped Japanese spring onion (*naga negi* / scallion)
Japanese seven-spice seasoning (*shichimi togarashi*) (optional)

Soak potato cubes in a bowl or pot of cold water to remove starch and avoid discolouration.

Stir-fry pork and vegetables in a pot over medium heat for 2–3 minutes until meat changes colour.

While soup is simmering, skim off any foam and scum that rises to the surface, using a small sieve, and discard.

Note: To save time when cooking, prepare an instant stock by dissolving 1$\frac{1}{3}$ tsp dashi powder in 800 ml (26 fl oz / 3$\frac{1}{4}$ cups) water.

Method

- Prepare dashi. Refer to method on p 16.
- Heat sesame oil in a saucepan and stir-fry pork, potatoes, carrot, white radish, devil's tongue jelly and burdock over medium heat for 2–3 minutes.
- Pour in dashi and simmer for about 10 minutes, then add shiitake mushrooms and bean curd.
- Simmer for 2–3 minutes, and skim off any foam that rises to the surface.
- Turn off heat, add sake and strain soy bean paste into soup, then stir until paste has dissolved.
- Add spring onion and reheat. When soup is almost boiling, remove from heat.
- Ladle soup into individual serving bowls. Garnish with sliced spring onion.
- Sprinkle seven-spice seasoning on top, if desired. Serve hot.

TOKYO-STYLE NEW YEAR'S SOUP (OZO-NI KANTO STYLE)

While rice cake soup is traditionally served on 1st January to celebrate the New Year in Japan, the recipe for the soup differs from region to region. This recipe hails from Tokyo, hence, its name.

Ingredients
Chicken thighs	120 g (4½ oz), skinned, fat removed and deboned, then cut into small pieces
Sake	1 tsp
White radish (*daikon*)	6-cm (2½-in) length, thinly sliced
Carrot	¼, peeled and cut into shapes with a vegetable cutter
Fresh shiitake mushrooms	2, stems discarded, shallow cuts made on mushroom caps to form desired pattern
Pink-swirled fish paste cake (*naruto*)	8 thick slices, each about 0.5-cm (¼-in)
Rice cakes	4, each about 50 g (2 oz)

Dashi (see Note)
Water	1 litre (32 fl oz / 4 cups)
Dried kelp (*konbu*)	12-cm (5-in) piece
Bonito flakes	30 g (1 oz)

Seasoning
Sake	1 Tbsp
Salt	½–⅔ tsp
Light soy sauce (*usukuchi shoyu*)	¼ tsp

Garnishing
Trefoil (*mitsuba*)	1 small bunch, cut into 2-cm (¾-in) lengths
Yuzu rind	1 small piece, cut into fine strips

Step-By-Step

Grill rice cakes in a toaster for 5–10 minutes until slightly puffy and brown on top.

With a sharp knife, peel a strip of yuzu rind and finely julienne. Avoid the white pith when peeling, as it has a bitter taste.

Place rice cakes in individual serving bowls, then ladle soup and ingredients over, this will allow the rice cakes to soak up the flavours of the soup.

Note: To save time when cooking, prepare an instant stock by dissolving 1⅓ tsp dashi powder in 800 ml (26 fl oz / 3¼ cups) water

Method
- Prepare dashi. Refer to method on p 16.
- Marinate chicken with sake and leave for about 10 minutes.
- Pour dashi into a medium-size pot and bring to the boil. Add chicken, radish, carrot, shiitake mushrooms and fish paste cake. Cook for about 10 minutes.
- While soup is boiling, grill rice cakes in a preheated oven at 200°C (400°F), or toaster for 5–10 minutes, until slightly puffy and light brown in colour.
- Mix seasoning ingredients together and stir into soup. Remove from heat.
- Place a grilled or toasted rice cake into each individual serving bowl and ladle soup over. Garnish with trefoil and *yuzu* rind. Serve hot.

SHORT-NECK CLAM CLEAR SOUP

(ASARI NO OSUMASHI)

Enjoy this clear soup with a rich-tasting stock, sweetened by the natural juices of the clams. You can also add seaweed, mushrooms and fish paste to the soup for a more substantial dish. If short-neck clams are unavailable, substitute with any other kind of clams.

Ingredients

Salt	1¼ tsp
Water	250 ml (8 fl oz / 1 cup)
Short-neck clams	300 g (10½ oz)
Sake	1 Tbsp
Light soy sauce (*usukuchi shoyu*)	1 Tbsp
Myoga ginger flower buds	2, thinly sliced

Stock

Water	700 ml (22 fl oz / 2¾ cups)
Dried kelp (*konbu*)	10-cm (4-in) piece

Step-By-Step

Soak clams in a large pot of cold salted water for 30 minutes; this helps to remove any sand and grit from clams.

Using a sharp knife, finely slice *Myoga* ginger flower buds along the grain on a chopping board.

Simmer clams in soup until their shells open; discard any that remain closed as they will not be properly cooked and may cause food poisoning.

Method

- Dissolve 1 tsp salt in water and soak clams for about 30 minutes to remove any grit. Rinse well, then drain and set aside.
- Prepare stock. Put water and kelp into a saucepan and leave for 30 minutes. Cook over medium heat and when small bubbles appear from the bottom, remove kelp.
- Heat stock in a medium saucepan and when boiling, add clams. Return to the boil, then reduce heat and skim off any foam that rises to the surface.
- Season with remaining salt, sake and light soy sauce. Simmer for 3 minutes, until clams open and discard any that remain closed.
- Ladle into individual serving bowls and garnish with sliced myoga ginger flower buds. Serve hot.

SIDE DISHES

Cucumber and Octopus Salad with Sweet Vinegar Dressing (*Kyuri To Tako No Sunomono*)

Deep-Fried Bean Curd (*Agedashi Tofu*)

Savoury Egg Custard (*Chawan Mushi*)

Simmered Hijiki Seaweed (*Hijiki No Nimono*)

Vegetables with Bean Curd Dressing (*Yasai No Shira Ae*)

CUCUMBER AND OCTOPUS SALAD WITH SWEET VINEGAR DRESSING

(KYURI TO TAKO NO SUNOMONO)

This is a refreshing and light salad with a non-oily dressing.

Ingredients

Japanese cucumbers	2
Salt	1 tsp
Boiled octopus tentacle	150 g (5$^{1}/_{3}$ oz), roll-cut into 2.5-cm (1-in) wedges
Old ginger	3-cm (1$^{1}/_{4}$-in) knob, peeled and finely shredded, then soaked in ice water and drained before use

Sweet Vinegar Dressing

Rice vinegar	3 Tbsp
Sugar	3 Tbsp
Salt	1 tsp
Light soy sauce (*usukuchi shoyu*)	$^{1}/_{2}$ tsp

Step-By-Step

Stir sweet vinegar dressing using clean fingers; the warmth from the fingers will help dissolve the sugar and salt in the mixture.

Sprinkle cucumbers with salt. Rub and roll them back and forth to smoothen and "scratch" the skin, enabling them to better absorb the vinegar dressing.

To roll cut the octopus tentacle, hold it firmly, then with the same hand, rotate the tentacle slowly as you slice it into wedges with a knife in the other hand.

Method

- Prepare sweet vinegar dressing. Put all ingredients into a small bowl and mix, using fingers, until completely dissolved. Set aside.
- Rub cucumbers with salt to smoothen skins, then rinse and cut into roll cut wedges.
- Chill sliced ingredients and dressing separately in the fridge until ready to serve.
- To serve, combine chilled cucumbers, octopus and seaweed in a salad bowl. Drizzle with sweet vinegar dressing and toss to mix well. Spoon onto individual plates and top with shredded ginger. Serve immediately.

DEEP-FRIED BEAN CURD
(AGEDASHI TOFU)

Bean curd is a very popular ingredient for Japanese cooking. It contains a lot of protein and is low in calories at the same time.

Ingredients

Bean curd (soft or firm)	2 slabs, each 300 g (10½ oz), cut into large pieces and pat dry
Egg	1, lightly beaten
Potato flour (potato starch) for coating	
Cooking oil for deep-frying	
Green *shishito* chillies	12, washed, pat dry and pierced
Light soy sauce (*usukuchi shoyu*)	1 Tbsp
Mirin	1 tsp

Dashi (see Note)

Water	150 ml (5 fl oz / ½ cup)
Dried kelp (*konbu*)	5-cm (2-in) piece
Bonito flakes	10 g (⅓ oz)

Garnishing

Finely sliced Japanese spring onion (*naga negi* / scallion)	to taste
Grated old ginger	to taste
Fine dried bonito flakes	to taste

Step-By-Step

Pierce a few holes in each *shishito* chilli to allow air to escape and prevent the chillies from bursting open during deep-frying.

Pat dry each piece of bean curd gently and thoroughly with absorbent paper before using. This ensures bean curd will be crisp when deep-fried.

Dip each piece of bean curd in beaten egg, then coat with flour and gently lower into hot oil. Deep-fry until light golden brown.

Note: To save time when cooking, make an instant stock for the soup by dissolving ¼ tsp dashi powder in 100 ml (3⅓ fl oz / ⅙ cup) water.

Method

- Prepare dashi. Refer to method on p 16.
- Dip bean curd pieces into beaten egg and coat with potato flour. Heat oil to 170°C (350°F) and deep-fry bean curd until golden. Remove and drain on absorbent paper.
- Scald shishito chillies in hot oil to preserve colour. Remove immediately and drain on absorbent paper.
- Prepare sauce. Heat dashi, light soy sauce and mirin in a small saucepan and bring to the boil. Remove from heat.
- Arrange deep-dried bean curd and shishito chillies in individual serving dishes and pour sauce over. Serve hot, garnished with spring onions, grated ginger and fine dried bonito flakes to taste.

SAVOURY EGG CUSTARD
(CHAWAN MUSHI)

In Japan, *chawan mushi* is prepared in traditional *chawan mushi* cups with lids. If you do not have these cups, use porcelain rice bowls or ramekins as substitutes.

Ingredients

Chicken thighs	50 g (2 oz), skinned and boned, fat removed and cubed
Sake	1 tsp
Salt	a pinch
Eggs	3, lightly beaten
Salt	1 tsp
Light soy sauce (*usukuchi shoyu*)	1 tsp
Prawns (shrimps)	8, large, peeled and deveined
Gingko nuts	8, shelled
Fresh shiitake mushrooms	2, stems discarded and finely sliced
Pink-swirled fish paste cake (*naruto*) or fish paste of choice	4 slices, each 0.5-cm (¼-in) thick
Trefoil (*mitsuba*)	4 stalks, finely sliced
Flower-shaped flour pieces for garnishing	

Dashi (see Note)

Water	600 ml (20 fl oz / 2½ cups)
Dried kelp (*konbu*)	8-cm (3¼-in) piece
Bonito flakes	20 g (⅔ oz)

Place the chicken, prawns, gingko nuts, mushrooms and fish paste cake neatly and attractively into each cup.

Strain egg mixture before using, so egg custard will have a silky smooth texture without bubbles after steaming.

Gently pour egg mixture into cups from a jug to ensure that cups are filled evenly.

Note: To save time when cooking, make an instant stock by dissolving 1 tsp dashi powder in 500 ml (16 fl oz / 2 cups) water.

Method

- Prepare dashi. Refer to method on p 16.
- Marinate chicken with sake and salt for 10 minutes.
- Mix together lightly eggs, salt, light soy sauce and dashi. Strain mixture using a fine sieve.
- Divide chicken, prawns, gingko nuts, shiitake mushrooms and fish paste cake equally among 4 heatproof (flameproof) cups or bowls.
- Gently pour an equal amount of egg mixture into each cup or bowl, then top with 1 flower-shaped flour piece.
- Cover cups with lids or aluminium foil if lids are unavailable; custard will have a smooth surface when steamed.
- Steam over high heat for 1 minute, then reduce heat to low and steam for about 12 minutes until egg mixture is set. Remove from heat and serve hot.

Soak hijiki seaweed in cold water for 20 minutes to rehydrate before using.

Place deep-fried bean curd on a flat metal sieve over a large bowl. Pour boiling water over to remove any oil. Drain well before use.

While ingredients are simmering in seasoned dashi, mix well with chopsticks to coat ingredients with sauce evenly.

Note: To save time when cooking, make an instant stock by dissolving ⅓ tsp dashi powder in 200 ml (6⅔ fl oz / ¾ cup) water.

SIMMERED HIJIKI SEAWEED
(HIJIKI NO NIMONO)

Hijiki seaweed contains a lot of calcium and is available dried, all year round. This popular side dish goes well with steamed rice.

Ingredients

Dark soy sauce (*koikuchi shoyu*)	4 Tbsp
Sugar	3 Tbsp
Mirin	2 Tbsp
Dried hiijiki seaweed	35–40 g (1–1½ oz), soaked for 20 minutes and drained
Deep-fried bean curd (*abura age*)	2, blanched and cut into long strips
Carrot	1, small, about 80 g (3 oz), peeled and shredded

Dashi (see Note)

Water	250 ml (8 fl oz / 1 cup)
Dried kelp (*konbu*)	5-cm (2-in) piece
Bonito flakes	10 g (⅓ oz)

Garnishing

Ground toasted white sesame seeds	to taste

Method
- Prepare dashi. Refer to method on p 16.
- Pour dashi, soy sauce, sugar and mirin into a medium saucepan. Bring to the boil and add seaweed, carrot and deep-fried bean curd. Reduce heat and simmer for 10–15 minutes, stirring occasionally, until most of the liquid is absorbed.
- Serve immediately or chill before serving, if desired.

Rinse blanched spinach under running water to remove any bitter taste and retain its colour and crunchy texture.

Wrap bean curd in a clean piece of muslin or cotton cloth. Squeeze gently to remove water. This will prevent the dressing from becoming watery later.

Place drained bean curd into a grinding bowl. Mash and grind with a wooden pestle to obtain a smooth mixture.

Note: To save time when cooking, make an instant stock by dissolving ⅓ tsp dashi powder in 200 ml (16 fl oz / 2 cups) water.

Step-By-Step

VEGETABLES WITH BEAN CURD DRESSING

(YASAI NO SHIRA AE)

In Japanese, *shira* means "white", while *ae* means "tossing". This dish is part of the vegetarian diet observed in Japanese Buddhist temples.

Ingredients

Spinach	70 g (2½ oz), roots discarded and washed
Sake	1 Tbsp
Light soy sauce (*usukuchi shoyu*)	1 Tbsp
Carrot	1, small, peeled and julienned
Dried shiitake mushrooms	4, soaked in warm water for 1 hour, stems discarded and finely sliced

Dashi (see Note)

Water	250 ml (8 fl oz / 1 cup)
Dried kelp (*konbu*)	5-cm (2-in) piece
Bonito flakes	10 g (⅓ oz)

Bean Curd Dressing

Bean curd (soft or firm)	1, 300 g (10½ oz), cut into small pieces and blanched
Sugar	2 Tbsp
Light soy sauce (*usukuchi shoyu*)	2 tsp
Salt	⅓ tsp
White sesame paste	5 Tbsp
Mirin	1 Tbsp

Method

- Prepare dashi. Refer to method on p 16.
- Blanch spinach in salted boiling water for a few seconds, then rinse under tap water. Drain well and cut into 4-cm (1¼-in) lengths. Set aside
- Pour dashi, sake and light soy sauce into a medium saucepan. Bring to the boil, add carrot and shiitake mushrooms, then reduce heat and simmer for 5–10 minutes until most of the liquid is absorbed. Drain simmered vegetables well. Set aside.
- Prepare bean curd dressing. Wrap bean curd in a clean piece of muslin or cotton cloth and squeeze gently to remove as much liquid as possible. Mash bean curd in a grinding bowl, then add remaining ingredients for dressing. Mix well and place in a salad bowl.
- Add spinach and simmered vegetables to bean curd dressing. Toss well and serve immediately.

VEGETABLES

Simmered Chinese Flowering Cabbage and Deep-Fried Bean Curd (*Komatsuna To Age No Nibitashi*)

Pan-Fried Aubergines with Miso Sauce (*Nasu No Nabeshigi*)

Simmered Lotus Root (*Renkon No Kimpira*)

French Beans with Sesame Dressing (*Ingen No Goma Ae*)

Simmered Pumpkin (*Kabocha No Amani*)

Simmered Radish with Minced Chicken (*Daikon No Soboro Ni*)

Simmered Vegetables and Chicken (*Chikuzen Ni*)

Cut Chinese flowering cabbage into 4-cm (1¾-in) lengths, separating the leaves and stalks

Halve each deep-fried bean curd lengthways, then slice crossways into long strips.

When simmering vegetables in soup, do not overcook as they will turn yellow.

Note: To save time when cooking, make an instant stock by dissolving ⅔ tsp dashi powder in 400 ml (13⅓ fl oz / 1⅝ cups) water.

Step-By-Step

SIMMERED CHINESE FLOWERING CABBAGE AND DEEP-FRIED BEAN CURD

(KOMATSUNA TO AGE NO NIBITASHI)

Nibitashi is a cooking method that involves simmering vegetables in soup.

Ingredients

Chinese flowering cabbage (*komatsu na*)	300 g (10½ oz), roots discarded
Deep-fried bean curd (*abura age*)	2
Sugar	2 tsp
Sake	2 Tbsp
Light soy sauce (*usukuchi shoyu*)	2½ Tbsp
Toasted white sesame seeds	to taste

Dashi (see Note)

Water	500 ml (16 fl oz / 2 cups)
Dried kelp (*konbu*)	10-cm (4-in) piece
Bonito flakes	20 g (⅔ oz)

Method

- Prepare dashi. Refer to method on p 16.
- Wash Chinese flowering cabbage and drain well. Cut into 4-cm (1¾-in) lengths, separating the leaves and stalks.
- Blanch deep-fried bean curd with boiling water to remove any smell and oil. Drain and halve each bean curd lengthways, then cut across into long strips.
- Add dashi, sugar, sake and light soy sauce into a medium saucepan. Bring to the boil, add bean curd strips and vegetable stalks, then simmer for 1–2 minutes until stalks are almost cooked.
- Add leaves and simmer for another 1–2 minutes. Remove from heat.
- Ladle soup into individual bowls and sprinkle sesame seeds on top, if desired. Serve hot.

PAN-FRIED AUBERGINES WITH MISO SAUCE
(NASU NO NABESHIGI)

When I was a child, my mother often prepared this dish for the family. A quick and simple recipe, it remains one of my favourite dishes today.

Ingredients
Japanese aubergines (nasu/eggplants)	6, washed, ends trimmed and cut into 1-cm (½-in) thick rounds
Cooking oil	3 Tbsp
Sesame oil	3 Tbsp
Toasted white sesame seeds	to taste

Seasoning
Soy bean paste (*miso*)	3 Tbsp
Sugar	3 Tbsp
Mirin	2 Tbsp
Sake	3 Tbsp
Water	2 Tbsp

Blend seasoning ingredients together in a small bowl with a mini whisk to obtain a smooth mixture.

Pan-fry aubergines on both sides until brown, turning the slices over with chopsticks.

Pour seasoning mixture evenly all over pan-fried aubergines. Cook until they are well-coated with thickened sauce.

Method
- Combine seasoning ingredients in a small bowl and blend well. Set aside.
- Heat both types of oil in a frying pan. Add aubergines and pan-fry for 3–5 minutes on both sides until brown.
- Pour seasoning mixture over aubergine slices, stirring gently to mix well. Simmer over low heat for 2–3 minutes until sauce has thickened and aubergines are well-coated. Remove from heat.
- Dish out onto a plate. Sprinkle sesame seeds on top, if desired, before serving.

SIMMERED LOTUS ROOT
(RENKON NO KIMPIRA)

A popular character in *Joruri*, a traditional Japanese play set during the Edo period, Kimpira is renowned for his superhuman strength. It is believed that eating this healthy dish will keep one strong like Kimpira, hence its name. If lotus roots are unavailable, substitute with burdock, carrots, potatoes or white radish.

Ingredients

Lotus root	200g (7 oz), washed and peeled
Dried red chilli	1, finely cut with a pair of scissors
Sesame oil	1 Tbsp
Toasted white sesame seeds	1 Tbsp

Seasoning

Dark soy sauce (*koikuchi shoyu*)	1½ Tbsp
Sugar	1 Tbsp
Sake	1 Tbsp
Mirin	1 Tbsp

Step-By-Step

Hold lotus root down firmly and slowly rotate it as you cut into long wedges with a sharp knife. Soak wedges as you cut, to prevent them from discolouring.

Blanch lotus root in water that is just boiling, to obtain a crunchy texture for the vegetable.

Add seasoning mixture to lotus root. Stir to mix well. Simmer for 1–2 minutes until coated with a glossy sauce, as shown in the picture.

Method

- Roll cut lotus root into wedges, then soak in water. Drain when ready to use.
- Bring a pot of water to the boil, then add drained lotus root and boil for about 5 minutes. Drain and set aside.
- Combine seasoning ingredients in a small bowl. Blend well until sugar has dissolved. Set aside.
- Heat sesame oil in a frying pan over medium heat, then add chilli and lotus root. Stir-fry for 1 minute.
- Pour seasoning mixture over lotus root and stir to mix well. Simmer for 1–2 minutes until most of the liquid is absorbed, and lotus root is well-coated with a glossy sauce. Remove from heat.
- Transfer to a plate and sprinkle sesame seeds on top before serving.

FRENCH BEANS WITH SESAME DRESSING
(INGEN NO GOMA AE)

Goma is the Japanese word for sesame seeds. This is a popular home-style side dish that is both delicious and easy to make. If French beans are unavailable, substitute with other vegetables such as spinach, carrots, burdock, lotus root, broccoli or aubergine (eggplant).

Ingredients
French beans	200g (7 oz), washed and trimmed
Black or white sesame seeds	6 Tbsp
Dark soy sauce (*koikuchi shoyu*)	2 Tbsp
Sugar	3 Tbsp

Step-By-Step

Spread blanched French beans on a bamboo flat sieve, and fan to cool and dry with a hand-held fan.

Toast sesame seeds evenly over low heat in a dry pan until aromatic. Stir occasionally to prevent sesame seeds from burning.

Place toasted sesame seeds in a grinding bowl and grind with pestle in a circular motion to obtain a fine mixture.

Note: To save time, or if you do not have a grinding bowl and pestle, you can use ready-ground sesame seeds, now easily available at many supermarkets. However, the ready-to-use product will not be as fragrant. Freshly ground sesame seeds also have a better flavour.

Method
- Blanch French beans in a pot of salted boiling water for 2–3 minutes. Drain in a flat sieve, then dry and cool by fanning vegetables with a hand-held fan, or plunge into ice water, then drain and pat dry.
- Cut French beans into 4-cm (1¾-in) lengths and set aside.
- Toast sesame seeds in a medium pan over low heat until aromatic.
- Transfer to a grinding bowl (*suri bachi*) and grind to obtain a fine mixture.
- Add soy sauce and sugar. Mix well.
- Transfer French beans to a large bowl. Toss well with ground sesame mixture.
- Dish out and serve immediately.

SIMMERED PUMPKIN
(KABOCHA NO AMANI)

Pumpkin is a summer vegetable with lots of vitamins. When buying pumpkins, choose those with bright orange-coloured flesh as they are sweeter. The vegetable is cooked very simply in this recipe, creating a very refreshing dish.

Ingredients

Japanese pumpkin	600 g (1 lb 5 oz), seeded, washed and left unpeeled
Water	250 ml (8 fl oz / 1 cup)
Sugar	2 Tbsp
Mirin	1 Tbsp
Light soy sauce (*usukuchi shoyu*)	1 tsp
Salt	a pinch
Toasted white sesame seeds	to taste

Step-By-Step

Bevel the edges of the pumpkin pieces on the skin side to help create a pretty pattern on the skin. This will also allow the vegetable to cook evenly.

Cover pumpkin completely with water, then place a drop-in lid or piece of paper over; this allows the pumpkin to poach evenly and fully absorb the seasoning.

Insert a skewer into a few pumpkin pieces to test if they are cooked. If the skewer pierces through the flesh easily, the pumpkin is ready.

Note: If the pumpkin pieces have to be simmered a little longer, and all the cooking liquid has evaporated, add more water as required.

Method

- Cut pumpkin into 5 x 6-cm (2 x 2½-in) pieces. Bevel the edges of each piece on the skin side.
- Put pumpkin, water and sugar in a medium saucepan, then cover with a drop-in lid, or a sheet of baking paper trimmed to fit pan. Simmer over medium heat for 2–3 minutes.
- Add mirin, light soy sauce and salt. Reduce heat to low and simmer for 5–10 minutes until pumpkin has softened. Remove from heat.
- Dish out, then sprinkle sesame seeds on top and serve.

SIMMERED RADISH WITH MINCED CHICKEN
(DAIKON NO SOBORO NI)

Radish is great for simmering in dishes with meat or poultry, as it can absorb the flavours of the other ingredients fully during the slow-cooking process. Turnips and pumpkins are also good substitutes for radish in this recipe.

Ingredients

White radish (*daikon*)	600 g (1lb 5 oz), peeled and cut into 2.5–cm (1-in) thick rounds
Raw rice grains (any kind except Basmati or fragrant Thai)	1 Tbsp
Salt	½ tsp
Light soy sauce (*usukuchi shoyu*)	½ tsp
Minced chicken	150 g (5⅓ oz)
Mirin	1 Tbsp
Sugar	1 Tbsp
Dark soy sauce (*koikuchi shoyu*)	1 Tbsp
Ginger juice	1 tsp
Potato flour (potato starch)	½ Tbsp, mixed with 1 Tbsp water
Old ginger	4-cm (1¾-in) knob, peeled, finely shredded, then soaked and drained before use

Dashi (see Note)

Water	500 ml (16 fl oz / 2 cups)
Dried kelp (*konbu*)	10-cm (4-in) piece
Bonito flakes	20 g (⅔ oz)

Step-By-Step

Gently score radish round with a cross. This will help the radish cook more quickly and evenly, and also help it absorb the seasoning more fully.

Boil radish with rice in water to remove its slightly pungent smell. Rice also removes the bitter taste of radish by absorbing its bitter juice.

When cooking the sauce, stir briskly with chopsticks to break up the minced chicken and prevent it from clumping together.

Note: To save time when cooking, make an instant stock by dissolving ⅔ tsp dashi powder in 400 ml (13⅓ fl oz / 1⅝ cups) water.

Method

- Prepare dashi. Refer to method on p 16.
- Bevel the edge of each round of radish on both sides. Make a cross-shape incision on one side of each round. Put radish and rice into a large pot, cover with water. Boil over medium heat for 20 minutes, until radish is cooked and just tender.
- Drain and discard rice and water, then rinse radish under tap water lightly to remove all bitter juices and rice starch. Drain.
- Add dashi, salt and light soy sauce into a large pot. Bring to the boil, then add cooked radish and simmer over low heat for 5 minutes. Remove radish from stock and set aside.
- Add minced chicken, mirin, sugar, dark soy sauce and ginger juice to stock. Mix well. Bring to the boil and stir in potato flour mixture to thicken sauce. Remove from heat.
- Divide radish among individual serving bowls and ladle sauce over. Garnish with shredded ginger and serve hot.

Tear devil's tongue jelly into small pieces, using your fingers; hand-torn devil's tongue jelly is able to absorb the seasoning more fully during cooking.

Stir-fry the vegetables and devil's tongue jelly for a few minutes, until well-coated with oil before adding mushrooms and chicken.

Cover with a drop-in lid, so that the ingredients are constantly bathed with simmering stock over evenly distributed heat, resulting in a full-flavoured dish at the end.

Note: To save time when cooking, make an instant stock by dissolving 1/3 tsp dashi powder in 200 ml (6 2/3 fl oz / 3/4 cup) water. Cutting root vegetables such as carrots and burdock into rolling wedges, helps expose more surface area of the cut pieces to heat, which allows them to cook more quickly and absorb sauces better during cooking.

SIMMERED VEGETABLES AND CHICKEN
(CHIKUZEN NI)

This dish originates from *Chikuzen*, a region in Japan, hence its name. It has now become a nationwide dish, and is often served during New Year celebrations.

Ingredients

Snow peas	12, trimmed and halved diagonally
Grey devil's tongue jelly (*konnyaku*) packed in water	120 g (4 1/3 oz) rinsed and drained
Cooking oil	1 Tbsp
Sesame oil	1 Tbsp
Lotus root	150 g (5 1/3 oz), peeled, cut into rolling wedges, soaked in water and drained when using
Burdock (*gobo*)	60 g (2 oz), peeled and roll cut into wedges, then soaked and drained before using
Carrot	100 g (3 1/2 oz), peeled and roll cut into wedges
Canned or boiled bamboo shoot	200 g (7 oz), roll cut into wedges
Dried shiitake mushrooms	5, soaked in 250 ml (8 fl oz / 1 cup) warm water for 1 hour, drained, stems discarded, cut into quarters; soaking liquid reserved
Chicken thighs	200 g (7 oz), cut into bite-size pieces
Sake	3 Tbsp
Sugar	3 Tbsp
Light soy sauce (*usukuchi shoyu*)	2 Tbsp
Mirin	1 Tbsp
Japanese seven-spice seasoning (*shichimi togarashi*)	(optional)

Dashi (see Note)

Water	250 ml (8 fl oz / 1 cup)
Dried kelp (*konbu*)	5-cm (2-in) piece
Bonito flakes	10 g (1/3 oz)

Method

- Prepare dashi. Refer to method on p 16.
- Blanch snow peas in salted boiling water for 1 minute. Remove and soak in ice water to refresh. Drain and set aside.
- Tear devil's tongue jelly into small pieces by hand. Blanch in boiling water for 1 minute to remove fishy smell.
- Heat both types of oil in a pot over high heat. Add all vegetables except mushrooms and snow peas.
- Stir-fry for 1–2 minutes, then add mushrooms and chicken. Stir-fry for another 1–2 minutes, until chicken changes colour and is cooked.
- Add dashi and mushroom soaking liquid. Bring to the boil and skim off any foam that rises to the surface.
- Add sake, sugar and light soy sauce. Cover with a drop-in lid and simmer over medium-low heat until liquid is reduced by half.
- Remove lid and add mirin. Cover and continue simmering until almost all the liquid is absorbed. Remove from heat, then add snow peas.
- Transfer to a large serving bowl. Serve hot, sprinkled with seven-spice seasoning, if desired.

Broiled Yellowtail (*Buri no Nabeteri*)

Grilled Spanish Mackerel with White Miso Paste (*Sawara No Saikyo Yaki*)

Salt-Grilled Horse Mackerel (*Aji No Shio Yaki*)

Simmered Mackerel in Grated Radish (*Saba No Mizore Ni*)

Simmered Red Snapper (*Tai No Nitsuke*)

Simmered Squid and Taro (*Ika To Satoimo No Nimono*)

Deep-Fried Seafood and Vegetables (*Tempura*)

SEAFOOD

Pan-fry fish fillets and spring onion together in a frying pan. Remove spring onion first and set aside as it browns more quickly than fish fillets.

Cover frying pan with a lid when pan-frying fish fillets to ensure even cooking, if fillets are thickly sliced.

Simmer until sauce is bubbling, glossy and reduced. The fish fillets and spring onion will be coated with sauce when ready.

Step-By-Step

BROILED YELLOWTAIL
(BURI NO NABETERI)

The Japanese-style cooking method of broiling, imbues any fish or meat with a fragrant soy sauce flavour. Feel free to substitute with other kinds of seafood such as Spanish mackerel, salmon and squid.

Ingredients

Cooking oil	1 Tbsp
Japanese yellowtail (*buri kirimi*) fillets	2, each about 100 g (3½ oz)
Japanese spring onion (*naga negi* / scallion)	½, cut into 4-cm (1¾-in) lengths
Ground Japanese pepper (*sansho*) (optional)	to taste

Seasoning

Dark soy sauce (*koikuchi shoyu*)	1½ Tbsp
Mirin	1½ Tbsp
Sake	1½ Tbsp

Method

- Combine seasoning ingredients and set aside.
- Heat cooking oil in a medium frying pan. Pan-fry yellowtail fillets and spring onion over medium-high heat.
- When spring onion is lightly browned, then remove and set aside.
- Cover, if required, and continue to pan-fry fish fillets for another 1–2 minutes, or until golden brown and crisp on both sides.
- Return spring onion to pan and add seasoning. Cook for another 1–2 minutes, until sauce is reduced, and fillets are well coated.
- Arrange fish on individual serving plates with spring onion. Serve, sprinkled with ground Japanese pepper, if desired.

*Pickled Lotus Root

Rice vinegar	5 Tbsp
Water	500 ml (16 fl oz / 2 cups)
Lotus root	200 g (7 oz)
Sugar	1 1/2 Tbsp
Salt	1/3 tsp

Method

- Prepare vinegar and water solution. Stir 1 Tbsp rice vinegar into water. Set aside.
- Wash and peel lotus root, then slice into 0.3-cm (1/10-in) rounds. Trim into flower shapes if desired. Soak in vinegar solution immediately for about 5 minutes to prevent discolouration.
- Drain and blanch in boiling water for 1–2 minutes until tender, but still crisp. Remove and drain well.
- Combine 4 Tbsp rice vinegar, sugar and salt until completely dissolved. Transfer mixture to a clean plastic bag and add lotus root. Seal and shake well. Refrigerate for at least 1 hour before use. Pickled lotus root can be kept refrigerated for up to 3 days.

GRILLED SPANISH MACKEREL WITH WHITE MISO PASTE

(SAWARA NO SAIKYO YAKI)

A local dish in Kyoto, the main seasoning ingredient used is white soy bean paste, or *saikyo miso*, a local speciality of the prefecture. The taste of this soy bean paste is sweeter than other varieties, and goes well with many kinds of seafood. Substitute Spanish mackerel with yellowtail, sea bream, salmon, squid, scallop or white promfret, if preferred.

Ingredients
Spanish mackerel fillets (*sawara*)	2, each about 100 g (3½ oz)
Salt	¼ tsp
Pickled lotus root*	

Marinade
White soy bean paste (*saikyo miso*)	100 g (3½ oz)
Brown soy bean paste (*mugi miso* or *shinshu miso*)	30 g (1 oz)
Mirin	1 Tbsp
Sake	1 Tbsp
Sugar	1 Tbsp

Sprinkle salt over fish fillets placed on a flat sieve over a large bowl. This will drain the fish of excess moisture.

Before grilling fish, pat dry with absorbent paper to prevent it from burning during cooking.

Cook fish on a hot grill pan, over medium heat on a gas hob. Grill on one side until brown, before turning it over to grill the other side. Be careful not to break fillet up.

Note: For convenience, marinate the wrapped fish fillets in advance, and store in the freezer for up to 3 weeks. The fish marinade can be stored and reused to marinate fresh batches of fish for up to 3 times. If preferred, other hardy root vegetables like white radish, carrot and turnip can also be used for pickling, in place of lotus root.

Method
- Prepare this dish at least 1 day ahead.
- Sprinkle fish fillets with salt and refrigerate for 30 minutes.
- Combine ingredients for marinade and set aside.
- Remove fish from refrigerator and pat dry with absorbent paper. Wrap fish in a clean piece of cotton gauze or muslin cloth.
- Put half the amount of marinade in a plastic container and place wrapped fish into container. Top with remaining marinade. Refrigerate overnight, or for up to 1 week.
- To cook, unwrap fish and pat dry with absorbent paper.
- Grill over medium heat, skin side first, for 2–3 minutes. Turn fish over and grill other side for 2–3 minutes until brown.
- Alternatively, grill fish fillets in a preheated oven at 200°C (400°F), skin side up, for 10 minutes. Turn fish over and grill other side for 5 minutes, or until brown.
- Arrange fish on individual serving plates. Serve hot with pickled lotus root on the side.

SALT-GRILLED HORSE MACKEREL (AJI NO SHIO YAKI)

Grilling is a popular cooking method for fish in Japanese cuisine. Many kinds of fish can be grilled including Spanish mackerel, bream, Pacific saury and sardine. Sardine and Pacific saury do not have to be gutted before cooking.

Ingredients
Horse mackerel (*aji*)	4, medium
Salt	1 Tbsp
White radish (*daikon*)	10-cm (4-in) length, peeled and grated
Dark soy sauce (*koikuchi shoyu*)	to taste
Lemon juice	(optional)

Garnishing
- *Oba* leaves
- Sliced lemon

Step-By-Step

On a piece of newspaper, trim and remove gills of each fish, using a pair of kitchen scissors.

Scrape away any hard scales at the joint of each fish tail, then make a long slit along the belly of each fish and scrape out the guts with the tip of the knife.

Carefully coat the fins and tails of fish with some salt. This keeps the fins and tails from getting burnt and disintegrating during grilling.

Note: Ensure that the grill is heated to smoking point before grilling, as the fish skin will stick to the grill if it is not hot enough.

Method
- Remove gills and gut fish, then rinse and pat dry with absorbent paper.
- Place cleaned fish on a flat sieve over a metal bowl to drain well.
- Just before grilling, sprinkle salt all over fish and coat tail and fins with salt.
- Heat a grill pan over medium heat on a gas hob until smoking, then grill fish on each side for 1–2 minutes until brown.
- Place grated radish in a fine sieve, then rinse briefly under tap water.
- Press radish with the back of a spoon to drain away bitter juice.
- Arrange fish, a small mound of drained radish drizzled with soy sauce to taste, oba leaves and lemon slices on a large serving plate.
- Sprinkle a little lemon juice over fish just before serving, if desired.

SIMMERED MACKEREL IN GRATED RADISH
(SABA NO MIZORE NI)

In Japanese, *mizore* means "sleet", while *ni* means "simmer". Grated radish resembles sleet, hence the Japanese name of the dish, "mackerel simmered with sleet".

Ingredients
Mackerel fillet	600 g (1 lb 5 oz), cleaned
Salt	½ tsp
Plain (all-purpose) flour	2 Tbsp
Cooking oil for deep-frying	
Sugar	1 Tbsp
Sake	3 Tbsp
Mirin	1 Tbsp
Dark soy sauce (*koikuchi shoyu*)	2 Tbsp
Grated white radish (*daikon*)	200 g (7 oz), drained of bitter juice
Spring onions (scallions)	2, cut into 4-cm (1¾-in) lengths

Dashi (see Note)
Water	125 ml (4 fl oz / ½ cup)
Dried kelp (*konbu*)	5-cm (2-in) piece
Bonito flakes	5 g (⅙ oz)

Step-By-Step

Pat dry each piece of fish thoroughly, then coat with flour, shaking off any excess. If fish is not properly dried, it will not be crisp when deep-fried.

Gently lower fish pieces into bubbling seasoned stock with cooking chopsticks, to avoid any splattering, and prevent fish from breaking up

Add drained radish into saucepan, and gently stir with chopsticks to mix well.

Note: To save time when cooking, make an instant stock by dissolving ¼ tsp dashi powder in 100 ml (3⅓ fl oz / ⅜ cup) water. If using salted instead of fresh mackerel, omit the salting stage and use directly.

Method
- Prepare dashi. Refer to method on p 16.
- Place mackerel on a flat sieve over a large bowl and sprinkle salt all over. Leave for 10 minutes to drain.
- Cut fish into large pieces and pat dry with absorbent paper.
- Heat oil for deep-frying to 180°C (350°F). Coat fish with flour, shaking off any excess. Deep-fry for 3–5 minutes, or until golden and crispy. Drain on absorbent paper.
- Add dashi, sugar, sake, mirin and soy sauce to a saucepan. Bring to the boil, then add deep-fried mackerel. Reduce heat to medium and simmer for 2–3 minutes.
- Add grated radish and spring onions and return to the boil. Remove from heat immediately.
- Transfer to a large serving bowl and serve hot.

Soak the shredded spring onion in ice water to curl them for better presentation as garnish.

Lower fish into pan, skin side up when seasoning liquid starts to bubble vigourously. Do not turn fish over in pan as it may break up easily.

When simmering, lift the drop-in lid or paper to spoon cooking liquid over fish regularly. This keeps the fish moist and helps it absorb the flavours more fully.

Step-By-Step

SIMMERED RED SNAPPER
(TAI NO NITSUKE)

Nitsuke refers to the Japanese cooking technique of simmering food in sake, sugar or mirin, and soy sauce. This cooking method is very popular for many kinds of fish including yellowtail, sardine, salmon and flatfish.

Ingredients

Burdock (*gobo*)	140 g (5 oz), washed and scrubbed clean
Water	200 ml (7 fl oz)
Sake	4 Tbsp
Sugar	3 Tbsp
Dark soy sauce (*koikuchi shoyu*)	3 Tbsp
Old ginger	4-cm (1³/₄-in) knob, peeled and sliced
Red snapper fillets (*tai*)	4, each about 100 g (3¹/₂ oz)

Garnishing

Japanese spring onion (*naga negi* / scallion)	¹/₂, white portion only, cut into 6-cm (2¹/₂-in) lengths

Method

- Cut burdock into 5-cm (2-in) lengths and quarter lengthways. Soak in water and set aside.
- Shred spring onion finely lengthways. Soak in ice water and set aside. Drain before use.
- Combine water, sake, sugar, soy sauce and sliced ginger in a medium frying pan and bring to the boil.
- When boiling, add burdock and place fish in the pan, skin side up. Cover with a drop-in lid, or a sheet of baking paper trimmed to fit pan.
- Simmer over medium-high heat for about 10 minutes, or until fish is cooked. Remove from heat.
- Arrange simmered fish on individual serving plates. Spoon some sauce over. Serve, garnished with simmered burdock and spring onion on the side.

SIMMERED SQUID AND TARO
(IKA TO SATOIMO NO NIMONO)

In Japan, the availability of *satoimo* taro at the markets heralds the beginning of the autumn season for many people. If *satoimo* is unavailable, substitute with unpeeled new potatoes, which are just as tasty. Frozen, ready-to-use *satoimo* can also be bought at many Asian supermarkets nowadays.

Ingredients

Satoimo taro	8, each about 60 g (2 oz)
Salt	1/2 tsp
Squid	1, about 300 g (10 1/2 oz), or 3–4 small squid, gutted and cleaned, then cut into 1-cm (1/2-in) thick rings
Dark soy sauce (*koikuchi shoyu*)	2 Tbsp
Sugar	2 Tbsp
Sake	2 Tbsp
Old ginger	4-cm (1 3/4-in) knob, peeled and cut into 0.3-cm (1/10-in) slices
Mirin	1 Tbsp

Dashi (see Note)

Water	400 ml (13 1/3 fl oz / 1 5/8 cups)
Dried kelp (*konbu*)	5-cm (2-in) piece
Bonito flakes	10 g (1/3 oz)

Step-By-Step

Hold squid down firmly on a chopping board and slice with a sharp knife into even rings.

In a mixing bowl, rub peeled taro with salt to draw out sticky juices. This will prevent the final dish from becoming starchy.

Add mirin to the pot during the last stage of cooking to obtain an attractive, glossy sauce.

Note: To save time when cooking, make an instant stock by dissolving 2/3 tsp dashi powder in 300 ml (10 fl oz / 1 1/4 cups) water.

Method

- Prepare dashi. Refer to method on p 16.
- Wash and peel *satoimo* taro, then rub with salt and rinse under tap water to remove sticky juices.
- Cover taro with water in a pot, then heat and bring to the boil. Continue boiling for another 2–3 minutes. Remove from heat, drain and set aside.
- Put soy sauce, sugar, sake, sliced ginger and dashi into a pot. Heat and bring to the boil, then add squid and taro and simmer for 15 minutes, or until taro and squid are very tender.
- Add mirin and simmer for 1–2 minutes, until heated through. Remove from heat.
- Transfer to a serving bowl and serve hot.

Dipping Sauce
Mirin	3 Tbsp
Dark soy sauce (*koikuchi shoyu*)	3 Tbsp

Dashi (see Note)
Water	250 ml (8 fl oz / 1 cup)
Dried kelp (*konbu*)	5-cm (2-in) piece
Bonito flakes	15 g ($1/2$ oz)

Method
- Refer to method on page 16 for preparing dashi.
- Put dashi, mirin and soy sauce into a saucepan, heat and bring to the boil for 1 minute. Remove from heat and transfer to individual sauce bowls.

DEEP-FRIED SEAFOOD AND VEGETABLES (TEMPURA)

Tempura originated from Europe about 400 years ago, but has become one of the most popular Japanese culinary delights in the world today.

Ingredients

Prawns (shrimps)	4, large, shelled and deveined, tails intact
Squid	1, about 200 g (7 oz) cleaned and cut into 3 x 4-cm (1⅓ x 1¾-in) pieces
Japanese aubergine (*nasu*/eggplant)	1, medium, halved lengthways, then cut crossways into 3 pieces
Carrot	1, small, peeled and cut into thick matchsticks
Sweet potato	½, peeled and cut into 0.7-cm (⅓-in) rounds, then soaked in water before use
Fresh shiitake mushrooms	4, stems discarded
Okra	4, medium, washed and pat dry
Oba leaves	4, rinse and pat dary
Japanese whiting (*kisu*)	4, small, gutted, cleaned and butterflied
Plain (all-purpose) flour	for dusting
Salt	to taste
Cooking oil	for deep-frying
Grated white radish (*daikon*)	150g (5⅓ oz), drained of bitter juice
Grated old ginger	10 g (⅓ oz)
Sea salt	(optional)

Batter

Ice-cold water	200 ml (7 fl oz)
Egg yolk	1
Plain (all-purpose) flour	125 g (4 oz), sifted

Step-By-Step

Using a sharp knife, carefully make 3 deep cuts, equal distance apart, along the belly of each prawn; this prevents it from curling when cooked.

Lightly fold flour into egg and water with chopsticks to form a lumpy batter. Use ice-cold water as it is essential for producing a light batter to make crisp and light tempura.

Deep-fry tempura in small batches, so that the temperature of the oil will remain constant and not result in a soggy and undercooked batter.

Note: To save time when cooking, make an instant stock by dissolving ⅓ tsp dashi powder in 200 ml (6⅔ fl oz /¾ cup) water. Instant tempura flour is available at most supermarkets; as it has a low gluten content, iced water is not required for a crisp batter.

Method

- Make 3 incisions across the belly of each prawn and straighten their bodies.
- Make a few diagonal slits on both sides of each piece of squid; this prevents them from curling when cooked.
- Make a few parallel cuts diagonally at one end of each piece of aubergine for it to spread out like a fan.
- Dust each kind of seafood and vegetable with flour lightly, except *oba* leaves.
- Prepare batter. Put water and egg yolk into a mixing bowl. Mix lightly. Using chopsticks or a fork, fold in flour lightly to form a lumpy batter. Do not beat.

- Heat oil to 170°C (340°F). Use a deep-fry thermometer to check temperature. Deep-fry vegetables first. Dip aubergine in batter and place in hot oil. Deep-fry 2–3 pieces at a time until crisp. Remove and drain on absorbent paper.
- Deep-fry carrot. Gather 4–5 matchsticks into a bunch each time, then dip in batter and fry in hot oil until crisp. Remove and drain on absorbent paper. Repeat with remaining vegetables in small batches until ingredients are used up.

- Heat oil to 180°C (350°F). Dip some prawns in batter and place in hot oil. Deep-fry in small batches until crisp. Remove and drain on absorbent paper. Repeat until remaining seafood is used up.
- Transfer tempura to a serving platter or traditional tempura basket. Serve crisp and hot, with bowls of dipping sauce. Mix small mounds of grated radish and a little ginger into dipping sauce when eating. Alternatively, dip tempura in sea salt instead of dipping sauce when eating, if desired.

MEAT & POULTRY

Braised Beef and Potatoes (*Niku Jaga*)

Braised Pork (*Buta No Kakuni*)

Japanese-Style Deep-Fried Chicken (*Tori No Tatsuta Age*)

Pan-Fried Ginger Pork (*Buta No Shoga Yaki*)

Deep-Fried Breaded Pork Cutlets (*Ton Katsu*)

Teriyaki Chicken (*Tori No Teriyaki*)

Soak potato chunks in cold water to remove excess starch and prevent discolouration. Drain just before using.

Hold carrot firmly on a chopping board with one hand, and slowly rotate carrot as you slice it into wedges with a sharp knife in the other hand.

Stir-fry onions and beef briefly with kitchen chopsticks. Mix well to prevent meat from clumping together.

BRAISED BEEF AND POTATOES *(NIKU JAGA)*

This recipe belongs to my mother and it is one of my favourites. Ask your local butcher for thinly sliced beef of a tender cut that is suitable for a simmered sukiyaki dish. Packaged sukiyaki-style beef is also available at the chilled section of most Japanese supermarkets.

Ingredients

Sesame oil	1½ Tbsp
White onions	1½, peeled and cut into wedges along the grain
Thinly sliced beef	200 g (7 oz), cut into bite-size pieces
Potatoes	4, medium, peeled and cut into chunks, soaked, then drained before use
Carrot	1, medium, peeled and roll cut into wedges
Hot water	300 ml (10 fl oz / 1¼ cups)
French beans	90 g (3 oz), trimmed and cut into 4-cm (1¾-in) lengths, then blanched

Seasoning

Sugar	1½ Tbsp
Mirin	1½ Tbsp
Dark soy sauce (*koikuchi shoyu*)	2½–3 Tbsp

Method

- Combine seasoning ingredients in a small bowl. Mix well and set aside.
- Heat oil in a pot over high heat, then add onions and beef and stir-fry for 1–2 minutes.
- Add seasoning and simmer briefly until all liquid is absorbed.
- Add potatoes, carrot and hot water. Cover and simmer over medium-high heat for about 15 minutes, until sauce is mostly absorbed.
- Stir in French beans and simmer for 1 minute to heat through. Remove from heat.
- Transfer to a serving bowl and serve hot with rice, if desired.

BRAISED PORK
(BUTA NO KAKUNI)

This delicious dish has Chinese origins, but has been adapted with Japanese seasoning ingredients to add a Japanese twist to the dish. I believe that it is also less fatty than the Chinese version.

Ingredients

Okra	12, washed and pat dry with absorbent paper
Salt	2 tsp
Pork belly	800 g–1 kg (1¾ lb–2 lb 3 oz)
Raw rice (any kind except Basmati or fragrant Thai)	2 Tbsp
Water	500 ml (16 fl oz / 2 cups)
Sake	200 ml (7 fl oz)
Mirin	100 ml (3⅓ fl oz)
Sugar	60 g (2 oz)
Japanese spring onions (*naga negi* / scallions)	2, green portion only
Old ginger	7-cm (3-in) knob, left unpeeled, scrubbed and cut into 0.5-cm (⅕-in) slices
Dark soy sauce (*koikuchi shoyu*)	4 Tbsp
Japanese hot mustard	(optional)

Step-By-Step

Pan-fry and constantly mop up any fat rendered from meat by pushing a piece of absorbent paper around the bottom of pan with tongs. Replace paper when soaked.

Add pork belly to a pot with water, sake, mirin, sugar and spring onions. Simmer, covered, for 30 minutes, until seasoning is fully absorbed.

The dish is ready when the sauce has reduced by half, and the pork belly pieces are coated with a layer of glossy dark sauce.

Method

- Sprinkle okra with salt, then lightly roll each okra on a chopping board with your hands to remove the fine hairs.
- Blanch okra in boiling water for 1–2 minutes, then remove and soak in ice water to refresh. Set aside.
- Heat a large pan and pan-fry pork belly over high heat until most of the fat is rendered and pork is lightly browned.
- Rinse pork with hot water to remove oil, then drain and cut into 5-cm (2-in) pieces.
- Place pork belly in a large pot and cover with water. Add rice and simmer over low heat for 2 hours until meat is completely tender. This will rid meat of any smell. Alternatively, simmer pork belly in a pressure cooker for about 20 minutes until tender.
- Remove meat and discard cooking liquid with rice. Rinse pork belly under tap water. Drain and set aside.
- Add 500 ml (16 fl oz / 2 cups) water, sake, mirin and sugar to a large pot. Bring to the boil.
- Add pork belly and spring onions, then lower heat and simmer with a drop-in lid, or baking paper trimmed to fit pot, for about 30 minutes. If using pressure cooker, simmer for 5 minutes.
- Remove and discard spring onions, and add ginger and soy sauce. Cover and continue to simmer for another 15–20 minutes, until sauce has reduced by half. If using pressure cooker, simmer for 3–5 minutes.
- To serve, drain and put okra into a deep serving dish. Transfer some pork belly to same dish. Add about ⅛ tsp Japanese hot mustard, if desired. Serve immediately.

JAPANESE-STYLE DEEP-FRIED CHICKEN
(TORI NO TATSUTA AGE)

This crispy chicken dish is absolutely delicious. It is popular with children and adults alike.

Ingredients

Boneless chicken thighs	500g (1 lb 1½ oz)
Dark soy sauce (*koikuchi shoyu*)	2 Tbsp
Sake	1 Tbsp
Mirin	1 Tbsp
Ginger juice	2 tsp
Potato flour (potato starch)	5 Tbsp
Vegetable oil for deep-frying	
Lemon wedges	

Step-By-Step

Marinate chicken in a large bowl for 30 minutes.

Pat dry chicken thoroughly with absorbent paper before coating with flour. This ensures that the fried chicken pieces are crisp and not soggy when deep-fried.

Coat chicken thoroughly with flour, making sure to shake off any excess.

Method

- Pierce each piece of chicken with a metal or bamboo skewer several times to enable meat to fully absorb seasoning ingredients. Cut into 4 x 5-cm (1¾ x 2-in) pieces and place in a large bowl.
- Marinate chicken pieces with soy sauce, sake, mirin and ginger juice. Set aside for about 30 minutes.
- Drain marinated chicken and pat dry thoroughly with absorbent paper.
- Coat with potato flour, shaking off any excess, then deep-fry in small batches in hot oil at 170°C (340°F) for 5–7 minutes, until brown and crisp. Drain on absorbent paper.
- Serve hot with lemon wedges on the side.

PAN-FRIED GINGER PORK
(BUTA NO SHOGA YAKI)

This is one of my favourite quick-and-easy recipes—I prepare it whenever I am pressed for time.

Ingredients

Pork tenderloin (fillet)	500 g (1 lb 1½ oz), cut into 0.5-cm (¼-in) thick slices
Sake	1 Tbsp
Dark soy sauce (*koikuchi shoyu*)	2 Tbsp
Mirin	2 Tbsp
Sake	2 Tbsp
Sesame oil	2 tsp
Sugar	2 tsp
Grated old ginger	2 Tbsp
Grated garlic	2 tsp
Cooking oil	1 Tbsp

Parsley Potatoes

Potatoes	2, medium, peeled and cubed
Finely chopped parsley	1 tsp
Ground black pepper	to taste
Salt	to taste

Garnishing

White radish sprouts	a small bunch, soaked in ice water and drained before use
Cherry tomatoes	2–3, halved

Step-By-Step

Toss potato cubes in a mixing bowl together with parsley, pepper and salt. Ensure that they are well-coated.

Blend seasoning ingredients for pork together with a mini whisk to obtain a well-blended mixture.

Add seasoning mixture to pork, then mix well with chopsticks. Simmer for 1–2 minutes more before removing from heat.

Method

- Prepare parsley potatoes. Boil potato cubes for 10–15 minutes until soft and cooked. Drain thoroughly and place in a mixing bowl. Sprinkle with chopped parsley, pepper and salt, then toss to mix well. Set aside.
- Marinate pork in sake for 5 minutes. In a small bowl, whisk together soy sauce, mirin, sake, sesame oil, sugar, ginger and garlic until well-blended. Set aside.
- Heat oil in a frying pan over high heat. Stir-fry pork briefly for 1–2 minutes, until meat changes colour.
- Add seasoning mixture to pan and simmer briefly for 1–2 minutes until pork is cooked. Remove from heat.
- Transfer to a serving plate. Arrange potatoes on the side and garnish with radish sprouts and cherry tomatoes. Serve with rice and a simple green salad, if desired.

Soak pork cutlets in milk and sake for 10 minutes to tenderise meat.

With a sharp knife, make a few cuts on each piece of pork between the fat and lean parts; this prevents meat from shrinking and curling up when cooking.

Dip flour-coated pork chops into beaten eggs, then coat with breadcrumbs. Press firmly with fingertips for breadcrumbs to adhere to meat.

Step-By-Step

DEEP-FRIED BREADED PORK CUTLETS (TON KATSU)

Although deep-fried breaded pork cutlets are commonly served at many Japanese restaurants, they are fairly simple to prepare at home.

Ingredients

Pork loin cutlets	4, boneless, each about 100 g (3½ oz), and 1.5-cm (¾-in) thick
Milk	125 ml (4 fl oz / ½ cup)
Sake	125 ml (4 fl oz / ½ cup)
Ground black pepper	to taste
Salt	to taste
Plain (all-purpose) flour	4 Tbsp
Egg	1, large, beaten
Dried breadcrumbs	55 g (2 oz)
Ground toasted white sesame seeds	4 Tbsp
Japanese hot mustard	to taste
Cooking oil for deep-frying	

Garnishing

Cabbage	300 g (10½ oz), finely shredded, soaked in ice water and drained before use
Tomato	1, cut into wedges
Cucumber	½, diagonally sliced
Lemon	½, cut into wedges

Sauce

Store-bought *tonkatsu* pork cutlet sauce	to taste
Ground toasted white sesame seeds	to taste

Method

- Marinate pork cutlets in milk and sake for about 10 minutes. Drain and pat dry with absorbent paper. Make a few deep cuts on each piece of meat.
- Tenderise cutlets briefly with a meat mallet, or the spine of a cleaver. Season with pepper and salt to taste.
- Coat each cutlet with flour, shaking off any excess. Dip into beaten egg and coat well with breadcrumbs.
- Heat oil to 160–170°C (325–340°F) Deep-fry pork cutlets, 1–2 pieces at a time, for about 5 minutes until golden brown.
- Remove and drain on absorbent paper. Repeat until all cutlets are deep-fried.
- Cut deep-fried cutlets crossways into 1.5-cm (¾-in) strips. Arrange on individual serving plates, accompanied by some cabbage, tomato and lemon wedges, cucumber slices and a dollop of Japanese hot mustard on the side, if desired.
- Serve hot, with individual bowls of ready-to-use *tonkatsu* dipping sauce, topped with ground sesame seeds.

TERIYAKI CHICKEN
(TORI NO TERIYAKI)

Teriyaki means "broil" in Japanese. Teriyaki sauce goes extremely well with mayonnaise.

Ingredients

Boneless chicken thighs	400 g (14 oz)
Cooking oil	2 Tbsp
Dark soy sauce (*koikuchi shoyu*)	2 Tbsp
Mirin	2 Tbsp
Sake	2 Tbsp
Mayonnaise	to taste
Ground Japanese pepper (*sansho*)	to taste

Garnishing

White radish (*daikon*)	1/4, peeled and finely julienned
White radish sprouts	1 small bunch, cut into 3-cm (1 1/4-in) lengths, soaked in ice water and drained before use

Step-By-Step

With a sharp knife, carefully make a few deep cuts in the thickest part of meat, being careful not to slice through skin. This allows chicken to cook through later.

While pan-frying chicken thighs, cover pan with a lid to allow the meat to cook faster and more evenly.

Simmer chicken thighs in bubbling sauce for a minute until well-coated, and sauce is reduced.

Method

- Trim and discard excess fat from chicken thighs. Make a few deep cuts in the thickest part of the flesh.
- Heat oil in a frying pan over high heat. Place chicken in, skin side first. Cover and pan-fry for about 2 minutes.
- Remove lid, turn chicken over and cover to pan-fry other side over medium heat for about 5 minutes, until brown and cooked.
- Combine soy sauce, mirin and sake in a small bowl, then pour sauce over chicken in pan. Cook for abour 1 minute until chicken is well-coated, and sauce is reduced. Remove from heat.
- Arrange chicken on a serving plate. Garnish with shredded white radish and radish sprouts as desired.
- Serve with mayonnaise on the side. Sprinkle chicken with ground Japanese pepper, if desired.

RICE & NOODLES

- Chicken and Eggs On Rice (*Oyako Don*)
- Cold Buckwheat Noodles (*Zaru Soba*)
- Deep-Fried Bean Curd Stuffed with Vinegared Rice (*Inari Sushi*)
- Mixed Rice (*Maze Gohan*)
- Sukiyaki Beef Bowl (*Gyu Don*)
- Red Rice (*Seki Han*)
- Thick-Rolled Sushi (*Futomaki Sushi*)

Slice halved onions into 0.7-cm (1/3-in) slices along the grain. This helps the onion slices to retain their shape and prevent them from melting during cooking.

Simmer chicken and onions in dashi and seasoning. Stir occasionally with chopsticks and cook until chicken meat turns white.

Gently pour beaten eggs from a jug into chicken and onion mixture, along the edge of the *oyako* pan. This allows the egg to set starting from the sides first.

Note: To save time when cooking, make an instant stock by dissolving 1/3 tsp dashi powder in 150 ml (5 fl oz / 5/8 cup) water. Use a small non-stick saucepan to cook the chicken and egg mixture, if you do not have an *oyako* pan.

Step-By-Step

CHICKEN AND EGGS ON RICE *(OYAKO DON)*

In Japanese, *oyako* refers to "parent and child", making reference to the use of chicken and eggs in this dish. This is popularly eaten for family lunches in Japan.

Ingredients

Boneless chicken thighs	400 g (14 oz), cut into bite-size pieces
White onions	2, medium, peeled
Eggs	6, lightly beaten and divided into 4 equal portions
Mirin	100 ml (3$\frac{1}{3}$ fl oz / $\frac{3}{8}$ cup)
Dark soy sauce (*koikuchi shoyu*)	4 Tbsp
Cooked Japanese short-grain rice	4 servings, kept warm
Trefoil (*mitsuba*)	1 small bunch, cut into 2.5-cm (1-in) lengths
Japanese seven-spice seasoning (*shichimi togarashi*)	(optional) or ground Japanese pepper (*sansho*)

Dashi (see Note)

Water	200 ml (6$\frac{2}{3}$ fl oz / $\frac{3}{4}$ cup)
Dried kelp (*konbu*)	5-cm (2-in) piece
Bonito flakes	10 g ($\frac{1}{3}$ oz)

Method

- Prepare dashi. Refer to method on p 16.
- Put 150 ml (5 fl oz / 5/8 cup) dashi, mirin and soy sauce into a medium saucepan. Bring to the boil, then add chicken and onions. Reduce heat to medium and simmer for 3–5 minutes, covered.
- Remove from heat and divide into 4 equal portions.
- Prepare a single serve of chicken and eggs on rice. Pour 1 portion of chicken and onion mixture into an *oyako* pan. Bring to the boil and pour in three-quarters of a portion of eggs.
- Cover and simmer for about 30 seconds over medium-low heat, then uncover and pour in remaining egg mixture. Cover and simmer for a few more seconds until mixture is almost set. Remove from heat.
- Gently slide chicken and egg mixture onto a serving bowl of rice. Garnish with trefoil and serve hot, sprinkled with seven-spice seasoning or Japanese pepper, if desired.
- Repeat cooking procedure with balance portions of chicken and onion mixture, and eggs to prepare remaining 3 servings. Serve as you cook, as the dish should be eaten hot.

COLD BUCKWHEAT NOODLES *(ZARU SOBA)*

Soba noodles make a very healthy dish as they have a high content of vitamin B and protein. Substitute with dried or frozen wheat (udon) noodles for a variation to this recipe.

Ingredients

Dried buckwheat noodles *(soba)*	400 g (14 oz)
Japanese spring onion *(naga negi / scallions)*	¼, finely sliced
Shredded dried seaweed *(kizami nori)*	4 Tbsp
Japanese seven-spice seasoning *(shichimi togarashi)*	to taste (optional)
Wasabi	to taste (optional)

Dipping sauce

Dark soy sauce *(koikuchi shoyu)*	3 Tbsp
Mirin	3 Tbsp

Dashi (see Note)

Water	250 ml (8 fl oz / 1 cup)
Dried kelp *(konbu)*	5-cm (2-in) piece
Bonito flakes	10 g (⅓ oz)

Step-By-Step

To prepare dipping sauce, combine dashi, soy sauce and mirin in a saucepan and bring to the boil.

Place noodles into pot only when water is boiling. Ensure there is plenty of water in the pot, or the cooked noodles will become overly starchy.

Rinse and rub the cooked noodles with your hands under running water to remove any starch and stop the cooking process. The noodles will then be crisp.

Note: To save time when cooking, make an instant stock by dissolving ⅓ tsp dashi powder in 200 ml (6⅔ fl oz / ¾ cup) water. Alternatively, use ready-made soba dipping sauce, which is available from Japanese supermarkets, and the Japanese goods section of any major supermarket..

Method

- Prepare dashi. Refer to method on p 16.
- Prepare dipping sauce. Combine 200 ml (6⅔ fl oz) dashi, soy sauce and mirin in a small saucepan. Bring to the boil, then remove from heat immediately. Set aside to cool completely.
- Bring a large pot of water to the boil. Add noodles and cook for 5 minutes, or until just tender (refer to cooking instructions on packet of noodles, if unsure). Drain noodles in a colander.
- Rinse and rub drained noodles for 1–2 minutes under cold running water. Drain well.
- Divide noodles among 4 individual serving plates. Sprinkle each plate with 1 Tbsp seaweed, spring onion and seven-spice seasoning, if desired. Divide dipping sauce among 4 bowls.
- Serve noodles with dipping sauce on the side, adding a dollop of wasabi to sauce, if desired.

Bean Curd Pockets

Deep-fried bean curd (*abura age*)	10, thawed before use if frozen
Dark soy sauce (*koikuchi shoyu*	4 Tbsp
Sugar	5 Tbsp
Sake	3 Tbsp
Mirin	3 Tbsp

Dashi (see Note)

Water	500 ml (16 fl oz / 2 cups)
Dried kelp (*konbu*)	10-cm (4-in) piece
Bonito flakes	20 g ($^2/_3$ oz)

Method

- Prepare dashi. Refer to method on p 16.
- Roll a chopstick over each bean curd and halve crossways. Carefully pull open cut ends to form pockets. Blanch with boiling water to remove excess oil.
- Put 400 ml (13 fl oz) dashi, soy sauce, sugar, sake and mirin into a medium saucepan. Heat and bring to the boil. Add bean curd, reduce heat to medium, and simmer, covered with a drop-in lid, or baking paper trimmed to fit pan. Cook until liquid has reduced by three-quarters.
- Add mirin and simmer for 2–3 minutes. Remove from heat and set aside to until cool. This allows bean curd to fully absorb the flavours of the seasoning. Transfer to a flat sieve and drain well before use.

DEEP-FRIED BEAN CURD STUFFED WITH VINEGARED RICE (INARI SUSHI)

Named after the Shinto god of rice, Inari, this sushi is traditionally presented as an offering to the god. According to legend, the pair of foxes that serve as the messengers of Inari have a fondness for deep-fried bean curd, hence the use of the ingredient in this dish.

Ingredients

Japanese short-grain rice	320 g (11½ oz)
Water	430 ml (14 fl oz / 1¾ cups)
Rice vinegar	60 ml (2 fl oz / ¼ cup)
Sugar	1 Tbsp
Salt	⅔ tsp
Toasted white sesame seeds	2 Tbsp
Toasted black sesame seeds	1 Tbsp
Thinly sliced pickled ginger (*gari*)	to taste

Step-By-Step

In a wet rice tub, "cut" a wet spatula down the centre, through the rice mixture, and fold rice over. Repeat "cut and fold" strokes, while fanning rice, to cool it rapidly.

Gently roll a chopstick over each bean curd, along its width briefly before halving; the bean curd pockets will open up more easily without tearing.

Stuff vinegared rice into bean curd pockets, ensuring hands are wet throughout the process. This prevents the rice from sticking to the hands.

Note: To save time when cooking, prepare an instant stock by dissolving ⅔ tsp dashi powder in 400 ml (13⅓ fl oz / 1⅝ cups) water.

Method

- Prepare rice for cooking. Put rice into a mixing bowl and fill with cold tap water. Stir quickly with fingers and drain. Press rice down repeatedly using your palm for 20–30 times to rub rice grains against one other. Refill bowl with tap water, then repeat the rubbing and rinsing process another 2–3 times until water almost runs clear.
- Leave rice to drain in a fine sieve for about 30 minutes. Transfer to a rice cooker. Add 430 ml (14 fl oz / 1¾ cups) water and turn on rice cooker. When cooked, fluff rice gently, using a wet Japanese spatula (*shamoji*). Set aside.
- Prepare sushi rice. Mix vinegar, sugar and salt in a small pot. Cook over low heat until fully dissolved.
- Transfer cooked rice to a damp wooden sushi tub or mixing bowl. Sprinkle vinegar dressing over while rice is still hot to give rice a glossy sheen.
- Fold rice with cutting strokes, and fan to cool at the same time. This prevents rice from clumping together. Do not mash.
- Mix in white and black sesame seeds.
- Cover tub or bowl with a clean wet cloth. Set aside.
- Assemble stuffed bean curd. Carefully open a bean curd pocket. Using wet fingers, stuff vinegared rice into pocket, leaving a 1-cm (½-in) margin from the edges. Press edges together and fold over to one side to seal pocket. Sit stuffed bean curd on folded edges to prevent it from opening up. Repeat until all ingredients are used up.
- Arrange stuffed bean curd on a serving plate. Serve, accompanied with thinly sliced pickled ginger to taste.

With a sharp knife, carefully trim away the ends of the mushrooms.

Rub rice grains against one another with your palm 20–30 times. Rinse and drain. Repeat this process 2–3 times until water almost runs clear.

Arrange carrot, chicken, mushrooms and bean curd in an even layer on top of seasoned rice.

Note: To save time when cooking, make an instant stock by dissolving ⅔ tsp dashi powder in 450 ml (22 fl oz / 2¾ cups) water.

MIXED RICE (MAZE GOHAN)

A wide variety of mixed rice dishes are available in Japanese cuisine. This dish is commonly packed into lunch boxes, or served for simple home meals and elaborate parties.

Ingredients

Japanese short-grain rice	320 g (11½ oz)
Short-grain glutinous rice	160 g (5½ oz)
Chicken thighs	150 g (5⅓ oz), boned and cubed
Sake	3 Tbsp
Dark soy sauce (koikuchi shoyu)	2 Tbsp
Salt	½ tsp
Carrot	1, peeled and julienned
Honshimeji mushrooms	130 g (4½ oz), ends trimmed
Deep-fried bean curd (abura age)	1, blanched, halved lengthways and cut crossways into long strips

Chicken Marinade

Sake	½ Tbsp
Dark soy sauce (koikuchi shoyu)	1 tsp

Dashi (see Note)

Water	500 ml (16 fl oz / 2 cups)
Dried kelp (konbu)	6-cm (2½-in) piece
Bonito flakes	15 g (½ oz)

Method

- Prepare dashi. Refer to method on p 16.
- Combine chicken cubes with ingredients for marinade. Set aside.
- Put both types of rice into a mixing bowl and fill with cold water. Stir quickly with fingers and drain. Press rice down repeatedly using your palm for 20–30 times to rub rice grains against one other. Refill bowl with tap water, then repeat the rubbing and rinsing process another 2–3 times until water almost runs clear.
- Soak washed rice in water for 30 minutes. Drain well.
- Transfer drained rice to a rice cooker. Add dashi, sake, soy sauce and salt. Mix well.
- Layer chicken, carrot, mushrooms and bean curd on top of rice. Turn on rice cooker to cook rice.
- When rice is cooked, fold mixture gently with a wet Japanese spatula (shamoji). Mix well.
- Transfer to individual serving bowls. Garnish as desired and serve hot.

SUKIYAKI BEEF BOWL
(GYU DON)

Sukiyaki is a popular seasoning sauce that usually comprises soy sauce, dashi, sake, sugar and mirin. Use beef belly for this dish, as its fat will melt during cooking and impart a wonderful flavour to the rice.

Ingredients

Cooking oil	2 tsp
Thinly sliced beef belly (*gyu bara*)	400 g (14 oz)
Dark soy sauce (*koikuchi shoyu*)	4 Tbsp
Sugar	3 Tbsp
White onion	1, large, peeled and cut into 12 wedges along the grain
Sake	4 Tbsp
Mirin	2 Tbsp
Cooked Japanese short-grain rice	4 servings, kept warm
Egg yolks	4
Pickled red ginger (*beni shoga*)	4 tsp
Chopped spring onions (scallions), green portion only	4 tsp
Japanese seven-spice seasoning (*shichimi togarashi*)	(optional)

Dashi (see Note)

Water	200 ml (6^2/$_3$ fl oz / ^{3}/$_4$ cup)
Dried kelp (*konbu*)	5-cm (2-in) piece
Bonito flakes	10 g (^{1}/$_3$ oz)

Step-By-Step

With a sharp knife, slice beef belly across the grain into 5-cm (2-in) wide pieces on a chopping board.

Gently pour combined mixture of soy sauce and sugar all over beef while stir-frying quickly with chopsticks.

After topping each bowl of rice with beef and onion mixture, gently slide an egg yolk into the centre of each bowl.

Note: To save time when cooking, make an instant stock by dissolving ^{1}/$_3$ tsp dashi powder in 150 ml (5 fl oz / ^{5}/$_8$ cup) water.

Method

- Prepare dashi. Refer to method on p 16.
- Cut beef belly crossways into 5-cm (2-in) wide pieces.
- Heat oil in a frying pan. Stir-fry beef for 1 minute.
- Combine soy sauce and sugar in a small bowl until dissolved. Add seasoning mixture to pan.
- Mix well. Cook for 1–2 minutes, then transfer to a plate and set aside.
- In the same pan, add dashi, sake and mirin. Heat and bring to the boil. Add onion and cook for 3–5 minutes until soft.
- Return beef to pan and heat through for 1–2 minutes. Remove from heat.
- Divide beef and onion mixture equally among 4 serving bowls of rice.
- Top the centre of each bowl with an egg yolk. Garnish each bowl with 1 tsp pickled red ginger and 1 tsp chopped spring onions.
- Sprinkle with Japanese seven-spice seasoning, if desired. Serve immediately.

RED RICE (SEKI HAN)

This is a traditional Japanese festive dish. It is often prepared and presented as a gift to relatives, neighbours and friends during special occasions such as birthdays and weddings.

ngredients

Japanese short-grain glutinous rice	480 g (12 lb)
Dried Japanese red beans (*sasage* or *azuki*)	60 g (2 oz), washed and drained
Water	600 ml (19$^{1}/_{3}$ fl oz / 2$^{3}/_{8}$ cups)
Toasted black sesame seeds	1 Tbsp
Salt	$^{1}/_{2}$ tsp

Step-By-Step

Cover red beans with water. Simmer for about 30 minutes, until beans are tender.

Pour strained liquid from cooking red beans into a measuring cup. Measure to obtain 300 ml (10 fl oz / 1$^{1}/_{4}$ cups) liquid. Top up with water if insufficient.

Place red beans, drained rice and cooking liquid in a rice cooker to cook.

Note: To obtain a more vibrant shade of reddish-pink for the rice, use Japanese red beans of the *sasage* variety.

Method

- Refer to method on p 89 to prepare rice for cooking. Soak washed rice in water for 30–60 minutes. Drain well.
- Cover red beans with water in a pot. Bring to the boil for 1–2 minutes. Drain well.
- Return drained beans to pot and add 600 ml (19$^{1}/_{3}$ fl oz / 2$^{3}/_{8}$ cups) water.
- Heat and simmer for about 30 minutes, until beans are soft.
- Strain mixture to separate red beans and cooking liquid. Measure 330 ml (11 fl oz) liquid to reserve for cooking rice. Discard any excess liquid, or top up with water, if amount is insufficient.
- Transfer drained rice, red beans and cooking liquid to a rice cooker and cook.
- When rice is cooked, fold mixture gently with a wet Japanese spatula (*shamoji*). Mix well.
- Transfer to serving bowls, or a traditional Japanese lacquer box. Sprinkle black sesame seeds and salt on top before serving.

Using chopsticks, lift and fold every newly set omelette over previous omelette to form a single multi-layered omelette.

Hold ingredients in line with fingertips and thumbs. Lift the edges of mat closest to you, to roll the ingredients up firmly.

When rolling western-style sushi, slip the bamboo mat in a resealable plastic bag before using. As the sushi is made with rice on the outside, the plastic cover prevents the rice from sticking to the mat.

Step-By-Step

THICK-ROLLED SUSHI
(FUTOMAKI SUSHI)

Sushi can be described as the most popular Japanese food in the world. This recipe features thick-rolled sushi that is commonly served in Japanese homes.

Ingredients
Laver (*nori*) sheets	10
Wasabi	to taste
Light soy sauce (*usukuchi shoyu*)	to taste

Sushi Rice (Vinegared Rice)
Japanese short-grain rice	960 g (2 lb 2 oz)
Water	1.15 litres (37 fl oz)
Rice vinegar	180 ml (6 fl oz / ¾ cup)
Sugar	3 Tbsp
Salt	2 tsp

Japanese-Style Filling
Broiled eel (*unagi*)	1, cut lengthways into long strips
Spinach	200 g (7 oz), trimmed to length of laver sheet and blanched in salted boiling water; refreshed with ice or tap water; then squeezed dry
Thinly sliced pickled ginger (*gari*)	to taste
*Rolled omelette	(see below)

*Rolled Omelette
Eggs	3, lightly beaten
Dashi	2 Tbsp (see page 16)
Sugar	3 Tbsp
Salt	⅓ tsp
Sake	½ Tbsp
Cooking oil	

Western-Style Filling
Toasted white sesame seeds	
Avocado	1, skinned, stoned and cut lengthways into long, thick strips
Cucumber	1, quartered lengthways and cored
Smoked salmon	200 g (7 oz), cut into long strips and trimmed to length of laver sheet
Crabsticks	4–6, halved and mixed with 2 Tbsp mayonnaise, salt and ground black pepper to taste

Method

- Refer to method on p 89 to prepare sushi rice.
- Prepare rolled omelette. Combine eggs, dashi, sugar, salt and sake in a bowl.
- Heat a greased rectangular omelette or non-stick pan. Pour one-fifth of the egg mixture into pan to thinly cover base. When omelette sets, fold in half towards you.
- Grease empty half of pan and push omelette to oiled part of pan. Pour another one-fifth of the egg mixture into empty part of pan, then lift the edges of the first omelette to allow egg mixture to run underneath, and replace.
- When second omelette is lightly set, fold it over the first. Repeat greasing, frying and folding procedure another 3 times to form a single multi-layered omelette at the end.
- Remove from pan and cool completely. Cut into 1.5 cm (3/4-in) wide strips.
- Assemble sushi with Japanese-style filling. Place a laver sheet on a sushi-rolling mat. Spread about 220 g (8 oz) cooled rice onto it lightly and evenly, leaving a 1-cm (1/2-in) margin along top and bottom edges.
- Make a shallow depression across the centre of rice. Wet fingers to prevent rice from sticking. Fill with some strips of omelette, eel, spinach and pickled ginger.
- Use mat to lift and roll laver and rice over filling firmly. Unwrap sushi roll, set aside and repeat to make 4 more rolls.
- Assemble sushi with western-style filling. Put sushi-rolling mat into a ziplock bag which fits nicely. Place a laver sheet on it. Spread about 220 g (8 oz) cooled rice onto it lightly and evenly to cover whole sheet. Sprinkle white sesame seeds all over. Press lightly but firmly to help sesame seeds adhere to rice.
- Turn laver sheet over on mat so that the surface with laver is now facing you.
- Line the centre of laver sheet with some strips of avocado, cucumber, smoked salmon and crabsticks.
- Use mat to lift and roll rice and laver over filling firmly. Unwrap sushi roll, set aside and repeat to make 4 more rolls.
- When all sushi rolls are ready, slice each roll crossways into 2-cm (1-in) pieces. Wet knife with rice vinegar or water after each cut; this ensures clean, neat slices.
- Serve with soy sauce and wasabi on the side for dipping, if desired.

Rice Balls with Red Bean Paste (*Ohagi*)

Candied Sweet Potatoes (*Daigaku Imo*)

Green Tea and Brown Sugar Buns (*Matcha To Kokuto Manju*)

Rice Balls Skewers (*Mitarashi Dango*)

Agar-agar, Glutinous Rice Balls and
Red Bean Paste with Syrup (*Shiratama Ann Mitsu*)

Pancakes with Red Bean Paste (*Dora Yaki*)

DESSERTS

Drain cooked red beans in a sieve, lined with a piece of muslin or straining cloth, then transfer red beans back to the pot for the next stage of cooking.

Simmer red beans with sugar over low heat, stirring constantly until paste thickens. Bean paste is ready when the bottom of the pot can be clearly seen when the beans stirred.

Shape rice balls using a sheet of plastic to prevent the sticky mixture from sticking to your hands.

Step-By-Step

RICE BALLS WITH RED BEAN PASTE (OHAGI)

We prepare *ohagi* and present them as a sweet offering to our ancestors during the week of the equinox.

Ingredients
Glutinous rice	320 g (11⅓ oz)
Castor (superfine) sugar	½ tsp

Soy Bean Powder Coating
Soy bean powder (*kinako*)	5 Tbsp
Castor (superfine) sugar	1 Tbsp

Red Bean Paste (*anko*)
Japanese red beans (*adzuki*)	500 g (1 lb 1½ oz), washed and drained
Japanese sugar (*jo haku to*) or castor (superfine) sugar	430 g (15⅓ oz)

Method

- Prepare red bean paste. Put red beans into a large pot and cover with water. Bring to the boil briefly, then remove from heat and drain.
- Return drained red beans to pot and add fresh water to fill up three-quarters of pot. Return to the boil, then reduce heat to low and simmer for 2 hours until beans are soft, skimming off any foam that rises to the surface. Remove from heat. Drain well.
- Return cooked red beans to pot and add sugar. Cook over low heat, stirring constantly for 10 minutes until paste thickens. Add salt and stir to mix well. Remove from heat.
- Spread out red bean paste on a baking tray. Set aside to cool.
- Divide cooled red bean paste into 20 equal portions, roll into balls and arrange on a baking tray. Cover with cling film (plastic wrap). Set aside.
- Refer to method on p 89 to prepare rice for cooking.
- Drain washed rice and transfer to a rice cooker. Top up with 430 ml (14 fl oz / 1¾ cups) water and soak for 30–60 minutes. Stir in sugar and turn on rice cooker.
- When rice is cooked, fold gently with a wet Japanese spatula (*shamoji*). Mix well. Using wet hands, divide rice into 20 equal portions and shape into balls. Place on a baking tray and set aside.
- Prepare red bean paste-coated rice balls. On a small sheet of plastic, place a ball of red bean paste and flatten into a 10-cm (4-in) round. Top with a rice ball and gently mould red bean paste around it to enclose. Shape to form a smooth ball, then remove cling film and set aside. Repeat to make 9 more.
- Prepare soy bean powder-coated rice balls. On a small sheet of plastic, place a rice ball and flatten into a 10-cm (4-in) round. Top with a ball of red bean paste and gently mould rice around it to enclose. Shape to form a smooth ball, then unwrap and set aside. Repeat to make 9 more. Coat each rice ball with soy bean powder, shaking off any excess.
- Transfer both types of rice balls onto a serving plate. Serve immediately.

CANDIED SWEET POTATOES
(DAIGAKU IMO)

Daigaku means "university" in Japanese. The origins of this dessert can be traced back to a shop, located in front of Tokyo University nearly a century ago, that sold these candied potatoes.

Ingredients

Japanese sweet potatoes	400 g (14 oz), scrubbed, rinsed and left unpeeled
Cooking oil for deep-frying	
Sugar	5 Tbsp
Water	2 Tbsp
Dark soy sauce (*koikuchi shoyu*)	1 tsp
Toasted black sesame seeds	1 tsp

Step-By-Step

Soak cut sweet potatoes in water for 10–15 minutes to remove excess starch, and any bitter aftertaste.

After sweet potatoes are cooked, pat dry to remove any moisture. This prevents the oil from splattering when sweet potatoes are deep-fried.

As the sauce will harden when it is cold, coat sweet potatoes in sauce evenly while it is still hot.

Method

- Cut sweet potatoes lengthways into 1.5 x 1.5 x 6-cm (¼ x ¼ x 2½-in) strips. Soak in water for 10–15 minutes. Drain.
- Cook sweet potatoes in the microwave oven on high, or steam over high heat for 5 minutes. Remove and pat dry. Set aside.
- Heat oil to 160–170°C (325–340°F). Deep-fry sweet potatoes for 2–3 minutes, until light brown.
- Remove and drain thoroughly on absorbent paper. Set aside.
- Combine sugar, water and soy sauce in a non-stick frying pan over medium heat.
- Stir continuously until sugar has dissolved completely. Continue to cook for another 2–3 minutes, until bubbles appear on the surface, and sauce has thickened and turned glossy. Remove from heat.
- Coat sweet potatoes with sauce evenly. Transfer to a serving plate. Sprinkle black sesame seeds on top and serve immediately.

GREEN TEA AND BROWN SUGAR BUNS
(MATCHA TO KOKUTOU MANJU)

Manju refers to "steamed buns" in Japanese. These sweet buns are usually served during Buddhist festivals and other happy occasions.

Ingredients

Brown Sugar Dough

Plain (all-purpose) flour	100 g (3½ oz)
Baking powder	1 tsp
Dark brown sugar	50 g (2 oz)
Warm water	50 ml (1⅔ fl oz)

Green Tea Dough

Castor (superfine) sugar	50 g (2 oz)
Warm water	50 ml (1⅔ fl oz)
Plain (all-purpose) flour	100 g (3½ oz)
Green tea powder (*matcha*)	1 tsp
Baking powder	1 tsp

Red Bean Paste (Anko)

Japanese red beans (*azuki*)	500 g (1 lb 1½ oz), washed and drained
Japanese sugar (*jo haku to*) or castor (superfine) sugar	430 g (15⅓ oz)
Salt	½ tsp

Step-By-Step

Gradually add flour to sugar solution. Combine and fold well with a spatula, scraping the sides of the bowl to obtain a smooth and sticky dough.

Divide rested dough into small portions. Weigh to ensure that each piece is about 20 g (⅔ oz).

Top a dough round with a portion of red bean paste. With a cupped hand, gather dough to enclose filling and seal. Shape into a smooth ball and flatten base slightly.

Note: Do not rest dough for more than 45 minutes as it will become very sticky and difficult to handle.

Method

- Refer to method on p 100 for preparing red bean paste. Divide cooled red bean paste equally into 20 balls, each about 25 g (⅚ oz). Place on a baking tray and cover with cling film (plastic wrap). Set aside.
- Prepare dark brown sugar dough. Sift flour and baking power together twice.
- Combine sugar and warm water in a mixing bowl and stir until dissolved. Cool completely. Gradually add sifted flour to sugar solution.
- Combine and fold mixture well to obtain a smooth and sticky dough. Cover bowl with cling film and set aside at room temperature for 30–45 minutes until dough firms up.
- Prepare green tea dough. Sift flour, and baking and green tea powders together twice. Repeat the same steps for making dark brown sugar dough. Set aside at room temperature for 30–45 minutes until dough firms up.
- Trim baking paper to obtain 20 pieces of 4-cm (1¾-in) squares. Set aside.
- Divide each batch of rested dough into 10 equal portions respectively, each weighing about 20 g (⅔ oz).
- Roll a piece of dough into a ball, and flatten into an 8-cm (3¼-in) round.
- Top with a portion of red bean paste, then gather dough to enclose filling and seal. Roll between hands to obtain a smooth ball, flatten base slightly and place on a square of baking paper. Repeat until ingredients are used up.
- Steam buns over high heat for about 10 minutes until cooked. Remove and serve warm.

Steam rice-flour dough in a preheated steamer lined with a piece of wet muslin cloth. This keeps the dough moist and prevents it from drying out.

Ensure that both the grinding bowl and pestle are wet when pounding and mashing the cooked dough. This prevents the dough from sticking to the bowl and pestle.

The metal grill should be red-hot before placing the sticks of rice balls onto it, to prevent the rice balls from sticking to the grill.

Step-By-Step

RICE BALL SKEWERS
(MITARASHI DANGO)

You can find this popular dessert at any traditional confectionery shop in Japan—it remains a perennial favourite of both the young and old.

Ingredients

Japanese rice flour (*jo shin ko*)	250 g (9 oz)
Sugar	1 Tbsp
Warm water	220 ml (7$\frac{1}{3}$ fl oz)
Bamboo skewers	10, soaked in water for 5 minutes and drained

Sweet Soy Sauce (Mitarashi Ann)

Water	100 ml (3$\frac{1}{3}$ fl oz)
Dark soy sauce (*koikuchi shoyu*)	70 ml (2$\frac{1}{3}$ fl oz)
Mirin	1 Tbsp
Sugar	90 g (3 oz)
Potato flour (potato starch)	15 g ($\frac{1}{2}$ oz), mixed with 15 ml ($\frac{1}{2}$ fl oz) water

Method

- Prepare rice balls. Combine rice flour and sugar in a mixing bowl. Add warm water and stir to mix well. Knead to form a medium-soft dough. Divide dough into 5–6 equal portions. Roll into balls and flatten into circles.
- Line the bottom of a preheated steamer with a piece of wet muslin cloth. Place dough circles into steamer. Cover and steam over high heat for about 15 minutes until cooked.
- Remove and transfer steamed dough circles into a wet grinding bowl (*suribachi*). Using a wet pestle, pound and mash dough circles together to obtain an elastic and soft dough.
- Divide and shape cooked dough into balls, each weighing about 15 g ($\frac{1}{2}$ oz).
- Skewer 3 rice balls on a bamboo stick. Repeat until ingredients are used up. Preheat a metal grill over a gas hob until red-hot.
- Grill each stick of rice balls for 3 seconds on each side until rice balls are seared with brown grill marks.
- Repeat until all rice balls are grilled. Set aside.
- Prepare sweet soy sauce. Combine water, soy sauce, mirin and sugar in a small saucepan.
- Heat and bring to the boil. Stir in potato flour mixture and cook until sauce has thickened and turned glossy. Remove from heat.
- Dip each stick of rice balls into sweet soy sauce to coat evenly. Serve warm.

Carefully remove set agar-agar from tin to avoid breaking it. Cut the agar-agar into small cubes.

Press the centre of each glutinous rice ball lightly with a finger to form an indent. The discs cook faster as heat is more evenly distributed this way.

Cook glutinous rice discs in boiling water until they float to the surface. Remove with a slotted spoon and drain.

AGAR–AGAR, GLUTINOUS RICE BALLS AND RED BEAN PASTE WITH SYRUP

(SHIRATAMA ANN MITSU)

Comprising a mouth-watering selection of textures, this dessert of chewy glutinous rice balls, smooth red bean paste and crunchy agar-agar cubes, laced with brown sugar syrup, is a real winner, and definitely my favourite. For an extra treat, serve with green tea ice cream.

Ingredients

Glutinous Rice Balls (Shiratama Dango)
Glutinous rice flour	150 g (5$^{1}/_{3}$ oz)
Water	130 ml (4$^{1}/_{6}$ fl oz / $^{1}/_{2}$ cup)

Agar-Agar
Water	600 ml (19$^{1}/_{3}$ fl oz / 2$^{3}/_{8}$ cups)
Agar-agar (*kanten*) stick	1, 7 g ($^{1}/_{3}$ oz)

Brown Sugar Syrup (Kuro Mitsu)
Muscovado (dark brown) sugar	100 g (3$^{1}/_{2}$ oz)
Water	50 ml (1$^{2}/_{3}$ fl oz / $^{1}/_{4}$ cup)

Red Bean Paste (Anko)
Japanese red beans (*adzuki*)	500 g (1 lb 1$^{1}/_{2}$ oz), washed and drained
Japanese sugar (*jo haku to*) or castor (superfine) sugar	430 g (15$^{1}/_{3}$ oz)
Salt	$^{1}/_{2}$ tsp

Garnishing
Canned mandarin orange slices	to taste
Canned cherries	to taste

Method

- Refer to method on p 100 for preparing red bean paste.
- Prepare glutinous rice balls. PLace glutinous rice flour and water into a mixing bowl. Combine well to form a smooth dough with a slightly sticky texture.
- Pinch off small portions of dough and roll into 2-cm ($^{3}/_{4}$-in) balls. Press the centre of each ball of dough with a finger to flatten into a disc with a slight indent.
- Bring a large pot of water to the boil and add glutinous rice discs. When they float to the surface, drain and transfer to a bowl of ice water. This prevents the sticky discs from clumping together. Set aside.
- Prepare agar–agar. Pour water into a medium saucepan and soak agar-agar stick for about 20 minutes, until soft.
- Bring to the boil for about 5 minutes, until agar– agar dissolves completely.
- Strain with a fine sieve. Pour strained mixture into a four-sided tin lined with cling film (plastic wrap).
- Leave at room temperature to set for 1 hour, then refrigerate to chill for 1 hour. When chilled, remove carefully and cut into small cubes.
- Prepare brown sugar syrup. Combine muscovado sugar and water in a small saucepan. Simmer over medium heat, skimming off any foam that rises to the surface, until sugar dissolves. Remove from heat. Pour into a serving jug and set aside to cool.
- To serve, place small portions of red bean paste, glutinous rice discs and agar-agar cubes into individual serving bowls.
- Garnish with mandarin orange slices and cherries to taste. Accompany with jug of brown sugar syrup for adding to taste.

Using an electric cake mixer, beat eggs and sugar together until very pale and thick.

Rest pan on a piece of damp cloth before pouring in batter. This helps to moderate the temperature of the pan, and prevents the underside of the pancake from getting burnt.

To assemble a *dora yaki*, spread 30 g (1 oz) red bean paste evenly on a pancake. Top with a few pieces of candied chestnuts, then sandwich with another pancake.

Step-By-Step

PANCAKES WITH RED BEAN PASTE (DORA YAKI)

Traditionally made up of red bean paste sandwiched between two pancakes, *dora yaki* takes it name from *dora*, the little percussion instrument of a gong that the snack resembles.

Ingredients

Plain (all-purpose) flour	100 g (3½ oz)
Baking powder	½ tsp
Eggs	2
Castor (superfine) sugar	90 g (3 oz)
Honey	1 Tbsp
Mirin	1 Tbsp
Water	2 Tbsp
Cooking oil for pan-frying	
Candied chestnuts	8, cut into small pieces

Red Bean Paste (Anko)

Japanese red beans (*azuki*)	500 g (1 lb 1½ oz), washed and drained
Japanese sugar (*jo haku to*) or castor (superfine) sugar	430 g (15⅓ oz)
Salt	½ tsp

Method

- Refer to method on p 100 for preparing red bean paste.
- Weigh cooled red bean paste to obtain 240 g (8½ oz) as filling for pancakes. Divide into equal portions of 30 g (1 oz) each, and arrange on a baking tray. Cover with cling film (plastic wrap). Set aside.
- Sift flour and baking powder together twice. Set aside.
- Beat eggs and sugar in a separate bowl until mixture is very pale and thick. Add honey, mirin and water. Combine well to obtain a smooth mixture.
- Using a rubber spatula spoon, gradually fold flour into egg mixture to obtain a smooth batter. Cover with cling film. Set aside at room temperature for about 20 minutes.
- Heat a little oil in a non–stick frying pan over low heat. Remove from heat and rest bottom of pan on a piece of damp cloth. Pour in about 3 Tbsp batter, then swirl pan to obtain an 8-cm (3¼-in) circle.
- Return pan to heat and cook over low heat for 1 minute, until bubbles appear on surface of pancake and underside is brown. Turn pancake over and pan-fry other side for a few seconds until brown.
- Remove cooked pancake and repeat to make more pancakes until batter is used up. There should be about 16 pancakes in total.
- Top half the pancakes, each, with a portion of red bean paste and some candied chestnut pieces. Sandwich with remaining pancakes. Serve warm or at room temperature.

GLOSSARY & INDEX

GLOSSARY OF INGREDIENTS

Agar-Agar (Kanten)
Agar-agar, or *kanten,* refers to a natural gelling agent that is derived from a fern-like seaweed that grows in the Pacific and Indian Oceans. Sold freeze-dried, agar-agar comes in three forms: sticks about 25 cm (10 in) in length, long filaments and powder. As agar-agar has no flavour or aroma, it is an excellent setting agent for cakes and desserts. Use as per instruction on the packaging for best results.

Bonito Flakes (Katsuo Bushi)
Shaved from smoked blocks of skipjack tuna, bonito flakes are one of the key ingredients, used especially for making the basic stock, dashi, in Japanese cooking. At the supermarket, there are several kinds of bonito flakes available. Large flakes called *hana katsuo,* are used for preparing dashi, while small flakes called *kezuri bushi* are used as a garnish for dishes. For optimum freshness, store them in the freezer.

Devil's Tongue Jelly (Konnyaku)
Derived from the roots of the devil's tongue, or *konnyaku* plant, which is part of the taro family, this dense, gelatinous cake has absolutely no calories. It is made by mixing *konnyaku* flour with water and then solidified, using lime water as a coagulant. Ranging in colour from black to mottled grey and greyish-white, depending on how refined the flour used is, the cakes or noodle-like strands are sold, packed in water. The jelly is very bland in taste, but is prized for its crunchy, gelatinous texture.

Bean Curd (Tofu)
Processed from soy beans, the ivory white bean curd has lots of textured vegetable protein, and being low in fat, is good for health. Bean curd is used in a wide variety of Japanese dishes, and there are basically two types available: soft bean curd (*momengoshi*) and silken bean curd (*kinugoshi*).

Soft bean curd is processed from soy bean milk mixed with a coagulant, that is then left to set in moulds lined with cotton cloth; this allows any excess water to drain away. The bean curd is therefore, firm in texture, and also has a visible cloth mark on its side when set.

Silken bean curd, on the other hand, is processed with thick soy bean milk, and set in moulds lined with silk. Hence the water content is retained, resulting in a bean curd with a smoother and softer texture.

Burdock (Gobo)
Rich in calcium and fibre, this thin, brown and long root was first introduced to Japan from China as a herbal medicine just before the 10th century. Cooked burdock has a stringy texture. As the nutritional content of the root lies just beneath its skin, do not peel, but simply scrub with a brush and rinse before using.

Deep-fried Bean Curd (Abura Age)
This thin, rectangular-shaped bean curd is highly versatile, and can be added to many dishes including stir-fries, simmered dishes and soups. Rich in vegetable protein, it can also be slit open to form pockets for stuffing with sushi rice or vegetables. Suitable for vegetarians, it is readily available, frozen or fresh, at Japanese supermarkets. Always blanch in boiling water before use to remove any excess oil.

Fish Paste Cake (Narutomaki)
In Japanese cuisine, fish paste cake usually refers to blended fish paste that is mixed with a binding agent, then steamed, boiled, grilled or deep-fried. *Narutomaki* refers specifically to a long slab of steamed fish cake that is decorated with a pink swirling pattern on the inside. It is a regular feature in Japanese noodle soups.

114

Green Tea Powder (Matcha)
This aromatic, bright green tea powder is made from steamed tea leaves which are dried flat and ground. Used in Japanese tea ceremonies, where it is whisked in hot water and drunk, green tea powder is also commonly used for making Japanese desserts.

Japanese Pepper (Sansho)
Although known as a pepper, *sansho* is not derived from a plant of the pepper family. Rather, it is processed from the seedpods of a tree belonging to the Japanese tangerine family. The seedpods are dried, with their seeds discarded, before they are ground into an intensely fragrant powder. The powder has a strong bitter flavour, and is used as a herb as well as a spice. Sansho leaves are used as a garnish, while the berries and dried berry skins are also used in daily cooking. In China, the dried seedpods are used as a spice, and known as Sichuan pepper.

Japanese Spring Onion (Naga Negi)
Ranging from 30–50 cm (12–20 in) in length, the Japanese spring onion resembles a slim leek, but is more similar in flavour to the smaller variety of spring onion. Favoured for its fresh, pungent aroma, the Japanese spring onion is often finely chopped and added to sauces or miso soups. It is sometimes also cut into short lengths, then grilled and served with grilled meats such as *yakitori* chicken.

Glutinous Rice Cake (Mochi)
Made from steamed and pounded glutinous rice, rice cakes are available in rectangular blocks, or circular shapes, and are usually eaten grilled, fried or lightly boiled. A traditional food, rice cakes are cooked in soups, and eaten by the Japanese to celebrate the New Year on the first of January. It is believed that the sticky and elastic qualities of the rice cakes symbolise long life and wealth. Ready-made rice cakes are easily available at Japanese supermarkets today, and if unopened, can be kept refrigerated for several months.

Japanese Red Beans (Azuki)
Rich in protein and fibre, Japanese red beans are regarded as a very nutritious food in Japan. Although used in both savoury and sweet dishes, red beans are predominantly used in making Japanese sweets, such as stuffed glutinous rice cakes (*mochi*) and glutinous rice balls (*ohagi*).

Honshimeji Mushrooms
This is a popular variety of Japanese mushrooms that grow in bunches under the Japanese oak and beech trees in the autumn. Cooked in clear soups and hotpots, these mushrooms are rather mild in flavour, but are highly regarded for their meaty texture. Before using, trim about 2.5 cm (1 in) of the spongy portion from the bottom, then rinse the mushrooms briefly under cold tap water, and gently separate into individual stems.

Kelp (Konbu)
An essential ingredient for preparing dashi, kelp is a seaweed with a fresh, intense aroma of the sea and is rich in calcium, calcium and fibre. It grows in the northern seas off the Japanese coast, and Hokkaido is its biggest producer. Kelp is available in various grades and sizes in the market, ranging from 5–30 cm (2–12 in) in width. When purchasing kelp, I recommend choosing those that are thick, and a glossy dark green in colour. Dried kelp is usually covered with a fine white powder that is a by-product of the drying process. Do not wash or rinse, but simply wipe with a piece of damp cloth before using. Kelp will last for several months refrigerated.

Oba (Shiso) Leaves
With a pungent fragrance reminiscent of that of basil's, *oba* or *shiso* leaves have been cultivated in Japan for centuries. They are often used as a garnish and herb for sashimi, tempura and salads.

Lotus Root (Renkon)
A popular root vegetable in Japanese simmered dishes, lotus roots are actually the rhizomes or stems of the lotus plant from which the roots grow. The stems are also sliced into thin rounds and pickled with vinegar to accentuate the sweetness of the vegetable. It has a refreshing crunchy texture and is best eaten during winter in Japan, when it is in season.

Mirin
An extremely sweet sake that is light golden in colour, mirin is brewed from glutinous rice and rice malt. Used in cooking, it imbues a dish with a subtle, sweet flavour, and an attractive glaze, and also goes well with soy sauce in many simmered dishes.

Myoga Ginger Flower Bud
This plant of the ginger family is cultivated for its edible flower buds and flavourful shoots, especially during the summer in Japan. With a piercing herbal aroma, the flower buds are often finely shredded lengthways, and added to dipping sauces, soups and vinegared vegetable dishes, or served with sashimi. The flowers buds are also soaked in brine and eaten as a pickled vegetable.

Noodles
Like rice, noodles are also a staple in the Japanese diet, and are often served for lunch. Made from a combination of buckwheat and wheat flour, soba noodles are rich in protein. Cold soba noodle are always served with a dipping sauce. Somen refers to very fine noodles made from wheat flour. The noodle dough is stretched very thinly with the aid of vegetable oil into really fine strands, and air-dried. Cold somen noodles are often served during the summer months in Japan. Udon refers to thick wheat noodles that are made from combining wheat flour with salted water. These thick noodles are available fresh, frozen or dried.

Rice

Short-grain rice, or *uruchi mai*, is a staple diet of the Japanese. It is served at almost every other meal in Japan. Although there are hundreds of varieties available, the most popular varieties are *sasanishiki* and *koshihikari*. Boiled or steamed, the Japanese short-grain rice is stickier and contains more moisture than long-grain rice varieties.

Glutinous rice has grains that are more opaque white than other types of white rice, and is probably the stickiest among all the rice varieties, when cooked. An example of a traditional Japanese dish that features glutinous rice is *sekihan* or Red Rice, where the sticky rice grains are cooked with red beans, and served during birthdays and other family celebrations.

Seaweed (Wakame/ Hijiki/ Kizami Nori)

An orangey-brown algae that grows on rocks in the sea during winter and summer, *wakame* seaweed is sold, dried or salted. Used in soups, salads and simmered vegetable dishes, dried, cut *wakame* is easily available at Japanese supermarkets today. Always soak the dried seaweed in water to rehydrate before using.

Hijiki seaweed is a black algae that grows around the coast of Japan, and is available in dried, narrow and curly strands. Like *wakame* seaweed, soak it to rehydrate before use. It is often combined with deep-fried bean curd (*abura age*) in simmered vegetable dishes.

Laver or nori sheets are sun-dried sheets of a film-like marine algae, that is greenish brown in colour. They have a slight smoky flavour and are used for wrapping sushi rice or adding to soups. Toast lightly before use to obtain a crisp texture and accentuate their aroma. *Kizami* nori refers to nori strips that are often added to soups, or rice dishes as a garnish.

Rice Vinegar

Light golden brown in colour, Japanese rice vinegar has a mildly sweet flavour that is less acidic than distilled white vinegar. In Japanese cooking, rice vinegar is used liberally to prevent food from discolouring, tone down salty flavours, and act as a natural preservative. An essential seasoning ingredient for making sushi rice, it is also used for preparing dishes like salads and pickled vegetables, including ginger and lotus root.

Sake

A very popular alcoholic beverage, and also a principal seasoning in Japanese cuisine, sake is brewed from rice, rice malt and water. There are practically thousands of kinds of sake available commercially today, although the best-quality sakes are probably produced on a small scale by family-owned breweries in Japan. Sakes made with well refined rice (until it is 60% of the original weight of the rice) are best drunk chilled because of their mellow fragrance, while others made from more processed rice (where the weight is at least 70% of the original weight of the rice) are drunk chilled or warmed.

When used in cooking, sake exudes a pleasant aroma that masks the strong smells of seafood and meat, and also helps ingredients to absorb seasoning well. Although sake brewed specifically for cooking is available nowadays, I prefer to use drinking sake, as it simply imparts a better flavour to the food.

Soy Bean Paste (Miso)

Used in soups, marinades and dipping sauces, soy bean paste or *miso*, is one of the most important seasoning ingredients in Japanese cuisine. As the paste is rich in protein, it was a precious and nourishing food in the olden days, when food was scarce.

The variety of soy bean paste differs from region to region, and are mainly categorised into three grades, according to the dominant ingredient that they are made with. Soy bean pastes made with rice are red, light brown or white in colour, and tend to have a mild flavour. Soy bean pastes made with barley are red or light brown in colour and have a medium flavour. Pure soy bean pastes are dark red or black in colour and have the richest and most salty flavour among the three. Another way of categorising soy bean pastes is by colour: white (*shiro miso*), red (*aka miso*) or dark (*kuro miso*).

A popular variety of soy bean paste is *shinshu miso*, a white soy bean paste made with rice, that hails from central Japan. I believe that the type of soy bean paste to use in any dish, is entirely one of personal tastes and preferences. As soy bean paste will lose its aroma if overcooked, add it to a dish only towards the end of cooking time. Always store any unused soy bean paste in tightly-covered containers in the fridge, to minimise the loss of flavour.

Seven-spice Seasoning (Shichimi Togarashi)

In Japanese, pure dried red chilli powder is known as *ichimi*. Seven-spice seasoning refers specifically to seven types of ground spices mixed together, namely, dried chilli powder, tangerine peel, poppy, sesame and hemp seeds, ground Japanese pepper and dried seaweed (*ao nori*). This condiment is usually sprinkled on top of soups, noodles, grilled meats and seafood, and rice bowls to give an extra oomph to the dishes.

Soy sauce

Salty in flavour, soy sauce is one of the essential everyday seasonings in Japanese cuisine, providing the dishes with both a pleasant flavour and colour. Two types of soy sauces are used for home cooking; dark soy sauce known as *koikuchi shoyu*, and light soy sauce known as *usukuchi shoyu*.

Used in dipping sauces and clear soups, light soy sauce is generally saltier than dark soy sauce, which is used in preparing simmered dishes. Store both types of soy sauces in the refrigerator for maximum freshness, after opening. Substituting Japanese soy sauces with their Chinese counterparts is not recommended, as they differ in aroma and flavour.

Trefoil (Mitsuba)

Mitsuba is a green leafy herb that belongs to the parsley family, but has more of a grassy scent, and a slightly bitter taste, compared to the usual parsley. It provides dishes like steamed egg custards (*chawanmushi*), and soups with a refreshing flavour.

Wasabi

Also known as Japanese horseradish, *wasabi* is a member of the cabbage family. The root of the plant is used as a spice. *Wasabi* has a pungent flavour and radish-like aroma. It grows naturally, along the beds of mountain streams flowing through river valleys in Japan. Although grating the fresh roots renders the best *wasabi* paste, they are rather rare, even in Japan. Instead, *wasabi* is more ready available in the form of powder and paste. In Japanese cuisine, *wasabi* paste is always served together with soy sauce to accompany sushi and sashimi.

Yuzu

This citrus fruit is about the size of a tangerine. It has thick, brightly coloured rind with a sharp, refreshing fragrance. *Yuzu* is used almost entirely for its aromatic rind. Small pieces are grated, or finely shredded, and added to soups, salad, pickles as well as desserts. Its juice is used to make a citrusy vinegar for salad dressings.

INDEX

A
abura age 19, 32, 38, 88, 90
Agar-agar, Glutinous Rice Balls and Red Bean Paste with Syrup (*Shiratama Ann Mitsu*) 108
all-purpose flour 61, 67, 78, 105, 110
aubergines 41, 67
azuki 95, 100, 105, 108, 110

B
Baised Pork (*Buta No Kakuni*) 73
bean curd 16, 29, 34
Bean Curd and Seaweed Miso Soup (*Tofu To Wakame No Misoshiru*) 16
beef 70, 92
bonito flakes 16, 19, 21, 29, 31, 32, 34, 38, 49, 50, 61, 65, 66, 84, 87, 88, 90, 92
Braised Beef and Potatoes (*Niku Jaga*) 70
Broiled Yellowtail (*Buri No Nabeteri*) 54
buckwheat noodles, dried 87
burdock 19, 50, 62

C
Candied Sweet Potatoes (*Daigaku Imo*) 103
carrot 19, 21, 32, 34, 50, 67, 70
chicken 21, 31, 49, 50, 75, 81, 84, 90
Chicken and Eggs on Rice (*Oyako Don*) 84
Chinese flowering cabbage 38
Cold Buckwheat Noodles (*Zaru Soba*) 87
Cucumber and Octopus Salad with Sweet Vinegar Dressing (*Kyuri Tako No Sunomono*) 26
cucumber, Japanese 26

D
daikon 19, 21, 49, 59, 61, 67, 81
dashi 16, 19, 21, 29, 31, 32, 34, 38, 49, 50, 61, 65, 66, 84, 87, 88, 90, 92, 96
Deep-Fried Bean Curd (*Agedashi Tofu*) 29
deep-fried bean curd see *abura age*
Deep-Fried Bean Curd Stuffed with Vinegared Rice (*Inari Sushi*) 89
Deep-Fried Breaded Pork Cutlets (*Ton Katsu*) 78
Deep-fried Seafood and Vegetables (*Tempura*) 67
Devil's root jelly 19, 50

E
egg/ eggs 29, 31, 78, 84, 96, 110

F
French beans 45, 70
French Beans with Sesame Dressing (*Ingen No Goma Ae*) 45

G
glutinous rice cakes 21
gobo see burdock
Green Tea and Brown Sugar Buns (*Matcha To Kokuto Manju*) 105
green tea powder 105
Grilled Spanish Mackerel with White Miso Paste (*Sawara No Saikyo Yaki*) 57

J
Japanese eggplants see aubergines
Japanese red beans see azuki
Japanese rice flour 106
Japanese spring onion 16, 19, 29, 54, 62, 73, 87

Japanese-Style Deep-Fried Chicken (*Tori No Tatsuta Age*) 75

K
kelp, dried 16, 19, 21, 22, 29, 31, 32, 34, 38, 49, 50, 61, 65, 66, 84, 87, 88, 90, 92
konnayaku see devil's root jelly
lotus root 42, 50, 56

M
matcha see green tea powder
mirin 29, 32, 34, 41, 42, 46, 49, 50, 54, 57, 61, 65, 66, 70, 73, 75, 77, 81, 84, 87, 88, 90, 92, 106, 110
miso 16, 19, 41, 57
Miso Soup with Pork and Vegetables (*Ton Jiru*) 19
mitsuba 21, 31, 84
Mixed Rice (*Maze Gohan*) 90
mochi see glutinous rice cakes
myoga ginger flower buds 22

O
oba leaves 59, 67
octopus tentacle, boiled 26
okra 67
onions, white 70, 84, 92

P
Pancakes with Red Bean Paste (*Dora Yaki*) 110
Pan-Fried Aubergines with Miso Sauce (*Nasu No Nabeshigi*) 41
Pan-Fried Ginger Pork (*Buta No Shoga Yaki*) 77
pink-swirled fish paste cake 21, 31
plain flour see all-purpose flour
pork 19, 73, 77, 78
potato flour 29, 49, 75, 106
potato starch see potato flour

potatoes 19, 70, 77
prawns 31, 67

R

Red Rice (*Seki Han*) 95
Rice Ball Skewers (*Mitarashi Dango*) 106
Rice Balls with Red Bean Paste (*Ohagi*) 100
rice vinegar 26, 56, 89, 96

S

sake 19, 21, 22, 31, 34, 38, 41, 42, 50, 54, 57, 61, 62, 65, 73, 75, 77, 78, 81, 88, 90, 92, 96
Salt-Grilled Horse Mackerel (*Aji No Shio Yaki*) 59
Savoury Egg Custard (*Chanwan Mushi*) 31
Scallion *see* Japanese spring onion
Short-Neck Clam Clear Soup (*Asari No Osumashi*) 22
short-neck clams 22
shrimps *see* prawns
Simmered Chinese Flowering Cabbage and Deep-Fried Bean Curd (*Komasutna Age No Nibitashi*) 38
Simmered Hijiki Seaweed (*Hijiki No Nimono*) 32
Simmered Lotus Root (*Renkon No Kinpira*) 42
Simmered Mackerel in Grated Radish (*Saba No Mizore Ni*) 61
Simmered Pumpkin (*Kobocha No Amani*) 46
Simmered Radish with Minced Chicken (*Daikon No Soboro Ni*) 49
Simmered Red Snapper (*Tai No Nitsuke*) 62
Simmered Squid and Taro (*Ika To Saitomo No Nimono*) 65
Simmered Vegetables and Chicken (*Chikuzen Ni*) 50

soy bean paste *see* miso
spinach 34, 96
squid 65, 67
Suyaki Beef Bowl (*Gyu Don*) 92
sweet potato 67, 103

T

Teriyaki Chicken (*Tori No Teriyaki*) 81
Thick-Rolled Sushi (*Futomaki Sushi*) 96
Tokyo-Style New Year's Soup (*Ozo-Ni Kanto Style*) 21
trefoil *see* mitsuba

V

Vegetables with Bean Curd Dressing (*Yasai No Shira Ae*) 34

W

white radish *see* daikon

Y

yuzu 21